**first-time mom's toddler discipline handbook**

# first-time mom's
# **toddler**
# **discipline**
## handbook

### Practical Advice and Go-To Strategies
### for Parenting with Confidence

Tara Egan, D.Ed.

ROCKRIDGE
PRESS

For general information on our other products and services or to obtain technical support, please contact our Customer Care Department within the United States at (866) 744-2665, or outside the United States at (510) 253-0500.

Rockridge Press publishes its books in a variety of electronic and print formats. Some content that appears in print may not be available in electronic books, and vice versa.

Interior and Cover Designer: Stephanie Mautone
Art Producer: Sue Bischofberger
Editor: Mo Mozuch
Production Editor: Mia Moran
Production Manager: Martin Worthington

All photography used under license © iStock and Shutterstock

Paperback ISBN: 978-1-64876-734-0 | eBook ISBN: 978-1-64876-735-7
R0

Calla Ruby and Natalie:
You're my favorite toddler
and toddler mom.
I love you both.

# Contents

# Introduction

Psst! Hi there! Yes, you with the tired eyes and the baby food on your shirt. I'm so glad this book made its way into your shopping cart, as I think I can help you navigate your child's toddler years with some practical advice and sincere encouragement.

Toddlerhood is no joke. Both you and your toddler are growing and changing *fast*. Every day is simultaneously more of the same (sleep, change diaper, eat, play) and completely different ("How did you scale that bookshelf while I was in the bathroom?").

I'm a mom, too, and not long ago, I was inundated with the challenges of teaching my little ones how to function in a world built primarily for grown-ups. I've had the privilege of coparenting with my husband, coparenting with that same man as my ex-husband, stepmothering while coparenting with an ex and a current partner, staying home with my children, balancing a career with motherhood, and parenting during a pandemic. I'm a former school psychologist, a child and adolescent therapist, a parent coach, a sometimes college professor, a public speaker, and a podcast host. I own a private practice that offers therapeutic and coaching services, plus I work with local educators and childcare providers. This is also my third parenting book!

In my professional life, I'm most often called on to support parents, particularly mothers. Mothers are constantly bombarded with messages that they aren't doing it as well as they should. Mothers are people, gosh darn it, and parenting a toddler who has big emotions, burgeoning motor skills, and developing language skills can be overwhelming. Moms need to stick together from day one.

I want this book to be a resource that you can consult when you feel like you need some words of encouragement and a helpful recommendation. This book will focus on understanding toddler behavior, managing day-to-day discipline, and fostering a sense of competence in you, Mama. I believe that every mom is exactly the right mom for their particular child, even if she wavers in her belief in herself during the tough moments.

One of the primary milestones that marks the transition from infancy to toddlerhood is the need to introduce discipline. Toddlers know how to try your patience, and they love flirting with the boundaries you've set. (I remember telling my son *not* to eat the dead flies off the garage floor. He definitely ate at least two after I said that.) This can cause uncertainty and confusion, as just when you think you've figured it out, your toddler develops a new skill or an unexpected response, and you're like, *Wait, now what?* Although parenting a toddler can feel isolating, all moms experience similar challenges. Learning strategies to deal with toddler behavior is important, but it's also essential that you feel confident enough to use them. This book will provide easy-to-implement exercises, tips, quotes, and real-life stories to inspire and encourage you and help fill your toolbox with useful parenting tools for the most challenging toddler moments.

That said, I recognize that not all toddlers develop in the same way, nor do they all respond the same to the best practices in parenting. Trust your mom instinct. If you're worried about either you or your toddler, reach out to a professional. Some examples that come to mind include moderate to severe anxiety or depression, developmental delays, or the feeling that one of you isn't physically or emotionally safe. This book is not a replacement for a therapist, medication, or medical treatment. If you have questions, reach out to your child's pediatrician, a mental health clinician, or an emergency resource, such as your local emergency department or a national hotline. There are resources in your community for all income levels, and it's 100 percent okay to use them. Believe me, asking for help is empowering; I've been there.

Motherhood can inspire joy and fear, sometimes both at the same time. Establishing a connected, emotionally responsive, consistent relationship with your toddler is key to not just surviving but flourishing during the toddler years. The two of you are a team, and I want you, as the leader, to feel calm and confident.

You've got this, Mama. Now let's get started.

# 1

# What Does It Mean to Be a First-Time Toddler Mom?

You're a first-time toddler mom! Welcome to an entirely new stage in your child's development. Take a moment now to appreciate reaching this milestone in your parenting journey. You've adopted or given birth to your first baby (or babies), and that baby has celebrated their first birthday and is developing new skills every day.

In this chapter, I'll focus on helping you understand the changes that your child and family are experiencing during this transition from infancy to toddlerhood. Developmentally, your child is able to understand and do more than ever before, and as a result, they're starting the long journey of slowly separating from you to become a fully formed person with their own personality, thoughts, and ideas. Experiencing this transition with your toddler is amazing but scary, especially as you try to guide them toward thinking, feeling, and behaving in a way that reflects your value system and hard work. I'll discuss this change, so you'll better understand what is going on with your little one and develop ways to cope with the uncertainty of it all.

> **"The most important thing she'd learned over the years was that there was no way to be a perfect mother and a million ways to be a good one."**
>
> —Jill Churchill

## Mom Moment

When my daughter was three years old, I took her to the dentist, which was located in a multistory building. I asked my toddler to remain at my side as I gave my payment to the receptionist. Across from the receptionist's desk was an elevator. As I chatted with the receptionist, relieved that our first dental appointment had concluded with only a few tears, I vaguely registered the chime of the elevator door. I glanced down and quickly realized that my toddler was no longer at my side. She had stepped on the elevator without me! We locked eyes as the doors slid closed. Her glee turned to dismay as she realized the doors were closing between us. I have never run down three flights of stairs so fast. I reached the bottom floor in time to find a woman holding my daughter's hand, asking, "Where's your mommy, sweetie?" Mom fail, big-time. At least I felt so at the time. What I didn't know then is that it wouldn't be the last time one of my toddlers completely unnerved me with unexpected behavior.

# Congratulations! You're a First-Time Toddler Mom

You did it! You and your child have conquered infancy, and you're careening toward toddlerhood. Friends and family might be murmuring about the upcoming "terrible twos," mentioning potty training, or inquiring about your plans for baby number two (*gulp!*), but I encourage you to take some time to reflect on how you've grown as a mom and how your bond with your child has blossomed in the past year.

## What Does That Mean?

Your child's transition from an infant to a toddler means that you're going to get to know a new version of your child—one who is more independent, curious, emotional, and expressive. Although it's amazing to see their personality emerge, it's also inevitable that you'll witness tantrums, variable moods, sassy words, risky behavior, and questionable social skills. Toddlerhood is not just an age; it's a stage of development. Although there can be considerable variability in skills from one toddler to the next—determined by both genetics and environment—there are some typical characteristics.

### Your Baby Is Growing Up

Toddlers, thankfully, retain nearly all of the sweetness of babyhood. They're affectionate, they often smell good, and they'll usually give you a bite of their cookie if you simply lean over and open your mouth. By now your toddler has taken their first steps, and they're making meaningful sounds and developing a distinct personality. The transition from infancy (0 to 12 months) to toddlerhood (about 12 months to 4 years) seems to happen in the blink of an eye. As your child grows up, it can sometimes feel as though you're just along for the ride.

## They Are Transitioning to a New Phase of Life

Toddlers can propel themselves, gather information using all five of their senses, learn primarily through playing and interacting with their environment and loved ones, and communicate with more and more ease. Because of these newfound skills, their world becomes bigger and more exciting. They are no longer completely helpless and dependent on a caregiver. Toddlerhood is a new phase of life, fostering autonomy and more advanced problem-solving skills. You can expect your toddler to embrace this new stage wholeheartedly (until they fall into bed exhausted each night).

## They Are Developing Intellectually, Socially, and Emotionally

Toddlerhood is often described as the stage during which children get into everything. They become little scientists, experimenting with how their body interacts with their environment and demonstrating the ability to complete multiple steps to get what they want. For instance, think about the toddler who wants the cookies in the cookie jar on the table. They know to pull out a chair, climb on it, open the jar, and reach inside. This is called means-end behavior. Toddlers recognize that objects exist even when they no longer see them (object permanence), and they love to imitate others and engage in make-believe play. Their skills develop gradually and are greatly enhanced by experience, which is why a four-year-old's cognitive skills far surpass those of an 18-month-old.

Emotional development begins at birth. When a mother sensitively and consistently responds to the cues of her infant, her baby learns that she is a secure, trusted person. As the baby reaches their first year, they typically demonstrate significant separation anxiety, exhibiting distress when separated from their primary caregiver. By the age of three, toddlers have learned that mommy always comes back and can tolerate exploring their world more independently. Toddlers who have formed a close, loving, responsive relationship with their primary caretaker are better able to extend the same skills toward others. Although parents of infants focus primarily on safety issues, parents of toddlers focus on appropriate social behavior, such as taking turns, sharing, and refraining from hitting. As you reinforce acceptable behavior and discourage unacceptable behavior, your toddler grows into a capable social being.

## They Are Becoming More Independent

Have you ever heard a toddler declare, "No! Me do it!"? If not, brace yourself. Toddlers will go to great lengths to try something without their parent's help or interference. I remember sinking to the floor in exasperation while waiting for my toddler to put on his own sandals, biting my tongue to keep from pointing out that they were on the wrong feet. Toddlers will squirm to be released from their parent's arms, creep out of their crib, swat their parent's hands away, slink out of sight, or simply cry or scream to gain autonomy. As a parent, there are times when you are 100 percent sure that a skill is beyond your toddler's ability level (your two-year-old will not be able to zip up their jacket or tie their shoes), but your toddler won't accept this until they've had a chance to try, fail, cry in frustration, and fail again. As a clinician and an educator, I adore their persistence. As a mom who has arrived late to many places due to this quest for independence, I have to coach myself to remain calm.

## They Are Becoming More Aware of the World around Them

If you haven't noticed already, you'll soon find that toddlers are observant. They can sense moods, notice when you're preoccupied by a phone call, and will consciously work to make a loved one laugh or smile. I remember my three-year-old son watching in awe as a group of high school boys played basketball at a neighborhood park. Later, I found him dodging around the living room, clumsily bouncing a ball and using exclamations like "Ova hah!" (Over here!) in an attempt to imitate the older boys. Your toddler's ability to imitate is growing exponentially. Although this is adorable, it means you have to recognize that your words, feelings, and actions are always being observed (and potentially imitated) by your curious little one, as any parent who has uttered a curse word in front of their toddler can attest.

## They Need You in a New Way

Although toddlers are no longer helpless infants, they still need you. Toddlers who have a healthy attachment to their parents view their parents as home base. They leave your side, explore until it feels uncomfortable or overwhelming, then return, ready for some affection, encouragement, or assistance. Your job as a toddler mom is to always be that secure place for them to have a soft landing after they've practiced being autonomous. This bond will serve your child well throughout their entire lifetime. Whether it's running to you after hearing a barking dog, burying their head in your shoulder after a long day in high school, or calling you as an adult to get your advice about a new car they want to buy, they'll always come back to you for reassurance.

## You Get to Watch Your Child Grow and Change

Some moms look back at their child's infancy and think, *Awww, they were so little! I miss those days.* Yet time marches on. I've always chosen to reframe my child's aging process as *They're getting so much cooler as they age!* They can stay up later, engage in more conversation, tell funnier jokes, and pee in the potty. It's a privilege to see a child tackle one task after another, and I enjoy being both a guide and an enthusiastic bystander. Parents need to understand that although they have a huge influence on how their child develops, there are some aspects of your kids that just *are.* Maybe it's a feisty personality or a tender heart. Maybe it's something that feels so very different from how you are. Whatever it is, they're still a little person you adore, and they adore you back, even when they're mad or sad.

# Your Toddler Will Challenge You Every Step of the Way

People are born with varying temperaments. Some people enter this world with a sunny disposition, are comfortable with change, and are resilient when stressed or disappointed. Others are slow to warm up, struggle to establish eating and sleeping routines, and have big, hard-to-regulate emotions. Depending on your toddler's temperament, their moods and behavior can feel relatively manageable, or you can feel like you're walking on eggshells. (Note: Too many eggshells suggest you should call a professional to get some support.) But you'll adjust, even in ways you never expected, in order to be the best parent for your child.

## A Mindfulness Exercise for When You Need a Minute

There are moments when having a toddler makes you close your eyes, press your fingers to your temples, and murmur, "How many minutes until bedtime? Seriously, the clock must be broken." A simple exercise I encourage mothers to do is to develop a mantra, a truthful, encouraging statement that inspires calmness and hope. Some of my favorite mantras, modified from posts from the Facebook page @RaisingTeensToday, are "It won't be this hard forever," "My toddler isn't giving me a hard time; he's having a hard time," or "I may not be able to control her moods or reactions, but I can control mine." Repeat your mantra, take several deep breaths, and spend some time stretching or enjoying the fresh air outside, and you'll have the stamina to make it to bedtime without any major meltdowns (from you or your toddler).

# Toddlerhood Won't Be Easy, but a Little Discipline Can Go a Long Way

Now that your little one is fully mobile, expanding their communication, and demonstrating their preferences via a firm head shake or a verbal "No," it's important that you begin to practice some simple ways to convey expectations to your toddler. Toddlers learn primarily by trial and error, but they don't have the forethought to anticipate consequences. It's up to you to observe their behavior and discipline them when necessary. This involves giving them feedback when they've made good and poor choices to send them the message "Good job! Keep doing that!" or "No, don't do that. Do something different next time." The goal of discipline is to shape your child's behavior so that they can express themselves in age-appropriate ways and follow sensible rules in their home and community. Even though toddlers have a reputation for having big emotions, some simple guidance from parents can ensure a more peaceful home.

## Discipline Can Help Strengthen Your Bond/Relationship

Kids crave structure. They are calmed by routine, comforted by predictability, and reassured by consistency. Because you are the mom and likely the person to whom your child is most connected, they're going to look to you to provide structure so that they feel safe and secure. Your toddler will thrive when you send consistent, gentle, clear messages about what behavior is acceptable and what behavior is unacceptable.

# Give Your Child and Yourself Time to Adjust

When you were expecting, experienced parents probably said things like "Get plenty of sleep now. You won't feel rested for years!" or "I couldn't find a spare moment to shower when my daughter was little. One time I didn't wash my hair for two weeks!" and you'd think, *Seriously? That can't be true.* But then parenthood happened, and it felt like plunging into an ice-cold bath on a hot summer day. By now you know that there are parenting moments that are impossible to prepare for in advance. Sometimes you need to live through an experience before you have any idea how to manage it in a competent way. Over time, you gain more practice dealing with the same issue, and it becomes easier to navigate. Think about the first time you took your baby out in public without your significant other to help. You were probably late, didn't bring the right supplies, and were super stressed when your baby cried in the car and you couldn't comfort her. By the tenth time you went out alone, you were more relaxed and felt prepared to deal with more circumstances. Give yourself time to adjust to the changes that toddlerhood brings, too. You'll get there.

## How to Handle Getting Easily Frustrated

Phew. Toddlers can be so . . . temperamental. One minute she's giggling over a game of peekaboo, and the next she's screeching because you dared to serve lunch on the red plate. You want your efforts to yield positive results, so it can be hard not to respond with a raised voice or a rough grasp. But remember that your toddler takes their cues from you. If you respond with a reasonable boundary, consistent consequences for misbehavior, and a calm voice, they're more likely to listen and understand. Here are some strategies to help you remain calm and positive when you feel like you want to erupt into your own tantrum:

- Step away from your toddler and take a deep breath. (It's very important to breathe in through your nose and out through your mouth. Seriously. Otherwise, you tend to pant and become more escalated. Try it first while you're calm.)
- Refrain from going into a frantic fix-it mode if your child is reacting unreasonably ("Do you want the pink plate? A cookie? A hug? A pony? Tell Mommy!"). You may have to wait until your toddler rides the wave of their emotions and then calmly redirect them to a new, more acceptable behavior.
- Dance it out. This may sound silly, but nearly everyone responds to music in a positive way. Play a funny song your toddler loves or one of your own personal favorites that gets you moving. Be careful you don't overwhelm your distressed toddler with the volume, and don't force them to dance if they don't want to, but do clap and laugh if they join in. Some fun tunes and exercise can be a great outlet for irritability.

# Remember, Change Is Hard for Everyone

Remember how I mentioned that kids crave structure? Well, so do moms. But because toddlerhood is not always predictable, you can end up experiencing whiplash when a nighttime routine you've always relied on is no longer effective or when your kid suddenly refuses to get out of the car when you pull up to day care. When this happens, take a breath and recognize that some parenting moments are hard. Although it's best to respond with a consistently calm demeanor and a problem-solving mindset, forces outside your control can override your best intentions. You'll need some strategies to default to when unexpected changes occur.

## Figure Out What Works Best for Your Family

A frequent morsel of advice I give to coparents is to divide child-care responsibilities based on likeability and success. Does one of you have more patience when it comes to dealing with a picky eater? Does the other enjoy splashing around at bath time? When it comes to the tasks you enjoy and feel competent at, it's okay to take the lead because you're more likely to feel relaxed and patient while doing them. When it comes to clipping toddler toenails, I'll pass, thank you very much. What works for one family may not work for another, so communicate with your coparent and support system, celebrate your successes, and my goodness, don't compare yourself to other moms on social media.

## Be Gentle

Stroke their hair. Rub their feet. Hold their hand even when there's no reason. Use sweet words and touch them gently. Even the most spirited and energetic child will benefit from this tender care. You'll see it reflected back when they interact with you, their friends, their teachers, and their pets. You will see a child who willingly makes eye contact, calms instead of storms, and gradually learns to modulate their words when frustrated or excited.

## Love Them Unconditionally

Sometimes my toddler would do something outlandish, and I'd think, *How is it that I'm raising a child who* _____. (See the anecdote in the introduction about my toddler son eating dead flies.) It's even more upsetting when your toddler does something that directly contradicts your belief system about what constitutes successful parenting. The thing is, no developmental phase, worrisome behavior, or insecure parenting moment is going to disrupt your unconditional love for your child or your investment in their well-being. They're yours, you're theirs. Always and forever.

## Have Fun along the Way

It's a weighty task, raising a toddler. Herculean, at times. They're probably going to cut their hair with an unattended pair of scissors, say something accurate but embarrassing in public, or wet the bed. But toddlers are snuggly, cute, and funny. It's important to enjoy their laughter and kisses, embrace the mess, and set aside your to-do list once in a while. One of the things that clients often say to me is that they're "not enjoying being a mom." Often when I look a little deeper, I find a mom who pressures herself to make every moment a learning moment, doesn't take time to foster an identity aside from being a mom, and frets about events that are unlikely (taking a peer's snack at day care is not a risk factor for them robbing a liquor store at age 17). Kids are fun. Moms can be fun, too. So, cut yourself a break and find the humor in the chaos. If you have a good sense of humor, your kid will likely have a good sense of humor, too. This comes in handy when it's time to laugh instead of cry.

## Let's Get Started

Reflect on what we've discussed in this chapter. Toddlers are always growing and changing. Understandably, so are your skills as a mother. You're developing a parenting style that works for you, your child, and your partner, and it's important to check in and ask yourself some questions:

- *Are our daily routines consistent and working for us?*

- *Is my child responding to me in a generally positive way?*

- *Am I treating my child in a gentle and respectful way?*

- *Am I accepting of who my child is?*

- *Do I permit my child to have age-appropriate autonomy so they can learn and grow?*

- *Am I managing my frustration and anxiety in a healthy way?*

- *Is our parent-child relationship based on security and trust?*

- *Am I taking care of myself as a parent and as a person?*

# Conclusion

In chapter 1, I provided you with some general principles of toddler development. The onset of toddlerhood is accompanied by significant changes in both the child and the mother. As toddlers explore their surroundings, expand their vocabulary, experiment with new behavior, and succumb to big emotions, it's important for moms to recognize that changes are to be expected, even if they're sometimes challenging. In chapter 2, I'll present you with some strategies for how you can care for yourself throughout this journey. A calm, healthy, supported mom = a more responsive, emotionally connected mom.

# 2

# You Are Doing the Best You Can

In this chapter, we'll focus on how toddlerhood impacts you, the mother. Sometimes motherhood is equated with self-sacrifice—as though you aren't working hard enough unless you're willing to come in dead last in the priorities of the household. Fatigue, a loss of sense of self, and under-stimulation do not equal a "good" mother. And really, why would you want to model that for your child?

Your goal is to recognize the all-consuming role of mothering a toddler so that you can harness the motivation to care for yourself. Mothers need support, both for themselves and for their toddler, to deal with the typical trials and tribulations as well the stress of the "yikes" moments. Mothers also need self-compassion, as they will inevitably make mistakes. Burnout is real and will significantly impact the joyful moments of motherhood and make the tough moments even harder. You matter, Mama.

> **"When you are a mother, you are never really alone in your thoughts. A mother always has to think twice, once for herself and once for her child."**
>
> —Sophia Loren

## Mom Moment

When my son was three years old, I desperately needed a haircut. It was summer, which meant that preschool wasn't in session. Armed with a bag of toys, a tub of snacks, and an optimistic attitude, I brought him with me to the hairdresser. The woman in the seat next to me offered her sympathy, remarking, "I hired a babysitter to stay with my daughter." I was dumbfounded. A sitter? To get a haircut? A routine task that was a nonessential self-care activity? She grinned at my surprise and said without apology, "I deserve a haircut and some highlights. Shoot, my kid gave me these gray hairs. She can hang out with our high school neighbor while I drink a cup of coffee and make myself look nice." It may sound silly, but it was a life-changing moment for me. I deserved to get a darn haircut free from the demands of a noisy toddler. Although I recognize that not everyone has the extra cash to pay a sitter or spring for a full head of highlights, everyone deserves to have their version of kid-free time.

## Being a Parent Is the Hardest Job of All

Kids are needy. They need to be fed, like, every day. They never want to sleep at the same time as their parents, and something is always sticky. Parents often report feeling more competent at their place of work than at home, and their parenting self-esteem always takes a hit when their child misbehaves, has an injury, or appears inexplicably unhappy. Sometimes it feels like parenting should be more formulaic: doing this + this + this = a happy, well-adjusted, successful child. Except it doesn't actually work that way. You can do everything "right" and never let your guard down, and you're still going to have a kid who struggles sometimes. So, it's important to pace yourself. Parenting is the hardest job of all. No parent can be "on" all the time and still have the stamina to persevere through the hard moments.

## Being a First-Time Mom Is a Wild Ride

When you're a first-time mom, you're doing everything for the first time. It feels like an experiment fueled by coffee and good intentions. I've heard parents jokingly refer to their first child as their "beta version" or "tester baby" because they felt like their experience of first-time parenthood consisted of 50 percent guesswork, 30 percent advice from parenting books, and 20 percent random content from the internet. And if you have a child who does not resemble the child described in the parenting books, it can be even more lonely and scary.

## You Are Constantly Adjusting, Stretching, and Accommodating Their Needs

As a toddler mom, one of your biggest challenges is having to constantly respond to your child's changing needs. When should you offer assistance, and when should you expect them to do it themselves? How much coaching should you provide when your three-year-old has a conflict during a playdate? Should you make them apologize when they do something wrong, or just suggest that they do so? Some of your decisions are made in the moment, and you might occasionally look back and think, *Why did I handle it that way?* You are constantly learning more about yourself and your child, and how you handle your child's needs will likely change over time.

## You Have to Set the Tone for Your Family

In my work with mothers and stepmothers, I constantly remind them that regardless of their experience with motherhood, they're nearly always the person in the home who sets the tone for the family. It may be the emotional tone, such as how emotions are expressed, what degree of emotional intensity is acceptable, or the preferred method of conflict resolution. It may also be the behavioral tone, such as determining what type of behavior is permitted (is it permissible to eat snacks in the playroom or to pile into Mom's bed on Saturday morning?) and what kind of behavior deserves consequences. Although you may verbally communicate the expectations, you also convey them via modeling, which is often more impactful. Here are some questions you can ask yourself when you're thinking about how you set the tone for your family:

- *Are you struggling to remain calm when you're upset?*

- *Can you hit the reset button in the afternoon after you've had a tough morning?*

- *Does your tone match your words?*

- *Do you follow through on what you say you'll do?*

- *Do your kids feel like your behavior is arbitrary and unpredictable or consistent and reasonable?*

You can't be expected to walk the line of amazingness all the time, but it's important to recognize that your actions and reactions set the precedent for how others think, feel, and behave.

## You Need Support and Structure Just Like Your Toddler

Coping with your toddler's needs can be stressful. Having some predictability in your own life, such as a consistent bedtime, regular meals, and opportunities to complete your adult responsibilities, can help you manage feelings of overwhelm. When I was a toddler mom, I benefited from a day that generally went like this:

- *Wake up, get dressed, and eat breakfast.*

- *Leave the house and do a toddler-friendly activity, such as a playdate, trip to the library, or an errand to a child-friendly store (like the grocery store that has the balloons).*

- *Come home, eat lunch, and take a nap.*

- *Do an activity within our home or neighborhood—play with the sprinkler, do a craft, go for a bike ride.*

- *Allow TV time during dinner prep, and then eat dinner.*

- *Take a walk as a family, spend some time outside in the yard, or clean up from the day.*

- *Take a bath, get into pajamas, read a story, and go to bed.*

Having some structure helped set the pace for the day. It set us up for success so that power struggles and meltdowns were minimal, but it allowed for flexibility when the weather was poor, a fun activity presented itself, or one of us didn't feel well.

## Take Time for You

Toddlers benefit from a consistent bedtime. I will talk about the nitty-gritty details later, but it's essential to understand that *parents benefit from their toddlers having a consistent bedtime.* You need to have a dedicated kid-free portion of your day. Although nap time might be a chance for some kid-free time, it is a guarantee in the evening if you're diligent about establishing a bedtime that is early enough to give you time to watch Netflix and chill.

## Five-Minute Self-Care Tips for Moms

*Self-care* is one of the most misused terms in American culture. Self-care is not always about bubble baths and a glass of wine; sometimes it's about taking time to recharge and feel a sense of calm.

Each year, I take an entire day off from work to do my taxes. I absolutely hate doing my taxes, and I feel completely defeated by the idea of coming home from a long day of work and spending my evening trying to balance parenting and taxes. So, I don't. I take a day off, get them done, and then feel like I'm crushing adulthood. It's my way of taking care of myself even though it's a dreadful task.

Although it's not always possible to take off an entire day from work, you can try to take five minutes here and there to do a few simple things:

- Take care of your body (wash your face, file that broken nail, find that cozy sweater you've been looking for).
- Take care of your living space (change your sheets, buy a new set of towels online, light a scented candle).
- Schedule something to look forward to (a playdate with your favorite mom friend, a therapy appointment, a date night, a haircut).

Self-care is about taking the time to focus on yourself and what you need, regardless of the task. You matter, too, Mama.

## Have Self-Compassion

One of my best friends accidentally locked her keys in her car while her toddler was asleep in the back seat. My friend panicked and immediately called the police, had them break the window, and sobbed into the phone to her husband while her baby continued sleeping, completely oblivious to the drama. She talked about that moment for years, only able to muster a chuckle when her kid entered middle school. After all this time, she still struggles to forgive herself for a moment of inattention that had little consequence other than the cost of a window repair. That was a hard day, one of many hard days as a mother. It's important to recognize that you're going to make mistakes. Most of them will be minor; some will be more serious. Although there is no perfect parent, you will occasionally fall victim to the falsehood that maybe you can be that exception if you just try hard enough. But that is extraordinary pressure to put on yourself and will likely result in you being unable to cut yourself a break, feeling afraid to ask for help, and encouraging perfectionism in your child. There is no perfect child, and there is no perfect parent.

## Stay Positive and Keep Learning

Throughout this chapter, I've mentioned the benefits of remaining calm and positive, especially during challenging moments. Toddlers can have volatile emotions, say mean things, and hit, kick, or bite. But getting mired in negative thoughts alters how you interact with your child. Sending yourself the message *I'm a bad parent, and my kid doesn't like me* can result in you feeling less compassionate and patient with yourself and your child, which is likely to escalate the situation. In contrast, if your self-talk is something like *My kid is trying to connect to someone or something in their world, and they're not sure how to do it. This isn't personal; it's developmental. We're going to get through this,* you're more likely to remain calm, coach yourself through managing your own emotions, and respond in a more loving, empathetic way. Each day is a new opportunity to learn and become even more connected to your child.

## Ignore the Critics and Mom Shaming

Other people will always have an opinion about how well you're doing as a parent. Whether it's a judgmental mother-in-law or a stranger on the internet, mothers are inundated with "shoulds" and "don'ts" and "why can't yous," which can rock your confidence, especially on the tough days. It can be hard to refrain from taking their words, sighs, or eye rolls to heart. When this happens, take time to remind yourself of these truths:

1. You're doing the best you can.

2. There is not a one-size-fits-all parenting approach.

3. What you do is rarely anyone else's business. Rock on, Mama.

## The Relationship between Thoughts, Feelings, and Behavior

During my work with parents, we often discuss the impact that thoughts have on feelings and behavior. Usually, if you reframe, or adjust, your thoughts, your feelings will become more uplifting and your behavior more positive.

**Example of negative thought:** Other moms are doing a better job than me. It comes more naturally to them.

**Resulting feeling:** *Discouragement, frustration, hopelessness*

**Resulting behavior:** *Negative attitude, impatience, becoming easily overwhelmed*

You can reframe this negative thought into something that is more positive but still truthful.

**Reframe of negative thought:** Parenting is really hard, and I'm doing the best I can. I need to focus on my strengths because I have many. I'm not alone in this, and my challenges are not insurmountable.

**Resulting feeling:** *Self-compassion, hopefulness, encouragement*

**Resulting behavior:** *Calm demeanor, brightened attitude, ability to take one step at a time*

It sounds a bit corny, I know. But reframing your negative thoughts into positive and encouraging self-talk makes it easier to focus on your parenting strengths rather than on the times you've faltered. Over time, your brain will do this automatically, and you'll avoid the dips in mood that come from not believing in yourself.

# Know When to Seek Support

As noted in chapter 1, not all toddlers develop cognitive, social, emotional, or behavior skills on the "typical" time line. Some toddlers demonstrate developmental delays in these areas:

- *Speech and language skills*
- *Fine or gross motor skills*
- *Cognitive abilities*
- *Emotional regulation*
- *Social skills*
- *Attention and concentration*

Additionally, some toddlers struggle with listening skills, compliance, sleeping, feeding, making eye contact, and aggression. For each one of those concerns, there are trusted experts in your community who can support you in helping your child reach their potential. Reach out, share your concerns, and ask for help. If a clinician feels your worries are unfounded, they'll let you know and educate you on what to look for in the future. I can't tell you how many times I've spoken to parents and given them hope by offering support and expertise. Parenting a child with worrisome behavior can be lonely, and it's hard to shift into problem-solving mode when you're getting crushed by the weight of handling it by yourself. Getting support will help you help your child.

## A Trusted Friend or Family Member

Oftentimes, parents first convey their concerns to a trusted friend or family member, usually someone they feel will listen closely, show compassion, and maintain their privacy. More frequently, however, parents are reaching out to online parenting groups, especially those that highlight a specific concern, such as "parents of children with asthma" or "parents of children with autism." Such groups can provide extensive information about symptoms and treatment, personal journeys, endorsements of professionals (both locally and nationally), or just general support and encouragement. Mothers will often feel closer to the other mothers in these online communities than to their real-life friends, as they know these other mothers "get it." Regardless of how and where you connect, it's essential that you feel heard and supported.

## A Child Development Specialist

Child development specialists might include developmental pediatricians, occupational therapists, physical therapists, speech and language therapists, special educators, social workers, audiologists, or physicians/physician assistants within a specific medical field, such as those who treat seizure disorders, pediatric acute-onset neuropsychiatric syndrome (PANS), genetic conditions, or other chronic health conditions. Specialists can be accessed through the public school system or the medical system and will often work as a team to support the child and the parents through the process of diagnosis, treatment, and follow-up care.

## A Psychologist or Therapist

A psychologist or therapist can help in a myriad of ways. They can support your child, you and your partner, or your entire family. They typically support family members via traditional talk therapy, behavioral management, play therapy, assessment, or consultation, and their training and experience vary.

It's essential to find the therapist who fits you—one you trust and feel confident is invested in your child and family and has the training and experience to support your child with their specific challenges. You can get referrals from friends, trusted professionals, or your health insurance, or you can google specific issues and carefully read online profiles and reviews, then schedule a virtual or in-person appointment. Therapists and psychologists are amazing resources and can completely transform your journey, but it's important to find the right one for you. I tell clients that finding a therapist is like dating—there are a lot of really great partners out there, but they're not all a good fit for you.

## Your Toddler Is Not Your Friend

I always need to take a deep, calming breath when I hear parents refer to their toddler as their "best friend," "little buddy," or "mini-me." Some might think, *Awww, that's so sweet*, but I think, *Oh, that sounds so lonely*. Toddlers are amazing, but they can't replace the company of an adult friend or partner. Parents with this mindset often unconsciously look to their toddler to meet their emotional or companionship needs, which is not age-appropriate, nor does it set the stage for a healthy emotional parent-child bond. It is too much pressure for a small child, as they are biologically programmed to grow up and away. Parents need to recognize that a toddler is on a developmentally appropriate quest to meet their own needs, not a parent's needs. Your job as a parent is to help your toddler regulate their emotions and behavior, learn to advocate for themselves, and treat others with respect so they can have close, age-appropriate connections with their loved ones. Parents also need to find ways to meet their own needs, separate from their relationship with their child.

## A Little Information Can Be a Big Help

Often parents reach out to me and indicate that they're unsure if their toddler's behavior is "normal." One activity I encourage parents to do is to keep some basic data about the frequency, duration, and intensity of their toddler's challenging behavior and see if it increases or decreases over time.

Frequency: *How often does the behavior occur? (Often measured in tally marks.)*

Duration: *How long does the behavior last? (Usually measured in minutes.)*

Intensity: *How severe is the behavior? How much does it disrupt your routine or the peace within your home? (Often measured on a scale of 1 to 5, with 5 being most severe.)*

Scenario 1: Malcolm's mother reports that Malcolm has frequent temper outbursts. After simple data collection for two weeks, we learn that Malcolm's tantrums occur one or two times per day, last three to five minutes, and are a 2 on the severity scale, as they rarely disrupt the routine, and Malcolm is typically able to regroup and have a positive day. His mother may briefly scold and feel frustrated, but she generally remains calm.

Scenario 2: Robert's mother reports that Robert has frequent temper outbursts. Data collection indicates that his tantrums occur about one time per week, last one and a half to two hours, and are a 5 on the severity scale (based on his mother's perception). Robert will often hit his mother, scream, wet his pants, and fall asleep for two to three hours afterward. Robert's mom usually calls her spouse, crying, and dreads seeing her son at the end of a workday.

Although both mothers express concerns about temper tantrums, Malcolm's and Robert's behavior are completely different, with Robert's behavior being more worrisome. Malcolm's mother felt reassured that his behavior was typical for a toddler and focused primarily on remaining calm and positive. In contrast, Robert's mother benefited from working with a child therapist to learn specific strategies to cope with Robert's underdeveloped emotional regulation.

# You Will Always Do Your Best for Your Child

Ask any mother, and they will tell you that they would do anything for their child, anything to make them happy, to reach their potential, to find love and be loved. Sometimes it can be hard to know what it means to "do your best," as a long-term goal can mean short-term discomfort for your child.

Here's an example: Your daughter has been warned to be kind to a peer while on a playdate. After she hits her peer for a second time, you decide to end the playdate and take her home. She screams in anger and embarrassment, and you feel miserable over the fact that she's so disappointed. But you've correctly decided that it's more important to set the standard that she show kindness toward others and not use aggression to solve problems rather than to appease her and inadvertently send a message that hitting others is acceptable.

Your version of "doing your best" means embracing that temporary distress. This can be really hard to do, especially if you feel your child doesn't quite understand your purpose or comprehend that their actions may be affecting someone else in a negative way.

# Conclusion

In chapter 2, I discussed some healthy behaviors that you should focus on as you weave your way through parenting an energetic, mischievous, and hilarious toddler. We focused on self-compassion, setting the tone for your family, assembling a support system, and remaining positive during challenging moments. All too often, moms ignore their personal well-being and end up feeling overwhelmed and ill-equipped. You're the queen of the castle, Mama. If you're not in good emotional and physical health, everything is harder. In chapter 3, I'll provide commonsense, easy-to-implement strategies for coping with the most common toddler challenges so you can fill up your parenting toolbox.

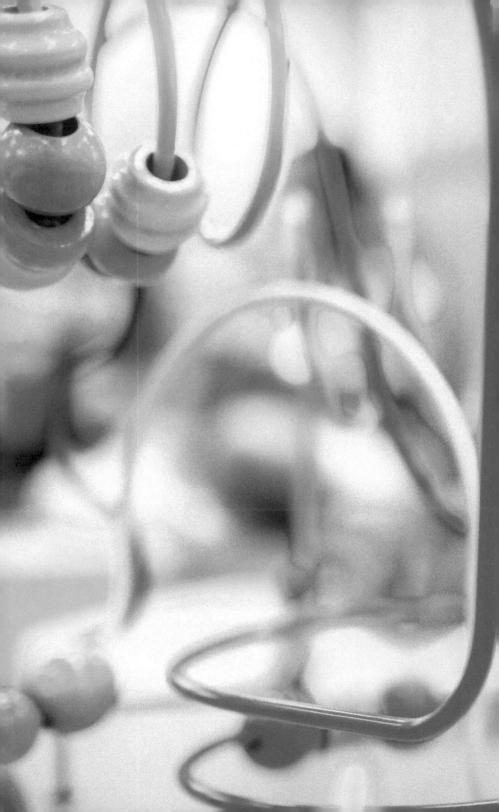

# 3

# Riding the Roller Coaster of Toddler Behavior

Strap yourself in, Mama. Toddlerhood is fun, but it's a little wild. Your toddler is going to challenge you like it's their job. Because it literally is their job. They're learning and growing and becoming more independent, which means that they're occasionally going to resist your well-intentioned guidance and protection, often in the form of tantrums and tears.

In this chapter, I'm going to describe some of the most common toddler mom challenges and offer recommendations to help you survive with as little drama as possible. Toddlerhood is eventful regardless of your effort and skill, but having a plan to deal with the tough moments can allow you to enjoy parenting your little one.

# "The easiest way to get your children to listen to you and to learn from you is by connecting with them first."

—Carolina King (*Mama Instincts*)

## Mom Moment

When my daughter was about three years old, she went to a neighbor's house for a playdate with a same-aged peer. My neighbor, Leah, is a dear friend and a wonderful mother. About an hour after the playdate began, Leah sent me a text that simply said, "One of our girls now has less hair. The other was found holding the scissors. Guess which one was holding the scissors?" I suspected her daughter was the scissor wielder because my daughter would never do that, obviously.

It turned out that my daughter was the self-proclaimed hairdresser, and her friend was missing one blonde pigtail.

**Follow-Up 1:** She did it again to her brother. He had a bald spot for weeks.

**Follow-Up 2:** My son then cut his own hair a few months later, also on my watch. We were working on a craft, and he just snipped off a chunk in about one second. I decided to take a break from scissors after the third incident, as I like to think of myself as a quick learner.

# The Most Common Toddler Behavior at Every Age

The educator in me wants to provide you with some common characteristics of toddlers at each age, but the therapist in me cringes a bit because I know how panicky new moms feel if their child hasn't reached a developmental milestone that has been described in a parenting book. The best way to combat flashes of worry is to form a trusted relationship with your child's pediatrician and facilitate an ongoing conversation about your child's behavior, skills, and struggles. Pediatricians are trained to monitor development and can refer you to a specialist if your child demonstrates a delay in physical, cognitive, or emotional development.

## Age 1 (ish) (12 to 24 months)

Between 9 and 15 months, children typically take their first independent steps. Their mobility is a game changer; they can move toward objects or people of interest, and their personality is more clearly discernible. Around this time, parents will start describing their toddlers as "social," "active," "timid," or "shy." By 18 months, toddlers can produce about 50 words. By 24 months, they can produce more than 200 words. Toddlers can understand more than they can say, and they can follow simple directions. Crying, screaming, and swatting are used to convey negative emotions, but you can usually distract them to ward off more lengthy temper outbursts.

# Age 2 (ish)

Researchers have determined that throughout infancy, babies experience feelings of joy, fear, and anger. Once they transition into toddlerhood and become more self-aware, more complex emotions emerge, such as embarrassment, pride, and shame. With emotional development comes parental expectations about socialization. By the age of two, parents are focusing less on safety and more on behaviors such as sharing, sitting still, and following adult directions. This transition is one factor that contributes to the frequent tantrums typically dubbed "the terrible twos." Parents might also notice their toddlers acting defiant, alternating between clinginess and independence, failing to wait their turn, and experiencing mood fluctuations. Toddlers over the age of two begin to show signs of empathy toward others, refer to themselves by name, and use feeling words like *sad* and *mad*.

# Age 3

Three-year-olds are blossoming in their language development, motor skills, and emotional regulation. They begin to develop self-talk, or inner speech, to coach themselves through a task or modulate their feelings. (I recall my three-year-old son sitting on the potty and whispering, "I can go pee-pee on the potty. My mommy loves me.") At this age, toddlers can use up to 500 words and phrases with two to six words. They can also imitate others and understand the difference between *mine* and *his*, *hers*, and *theirs*. Some toddlers will also ask at least 2,645 questions per day. Most toddlers will become daytime potty-trained between two and a half and three and half years old, with some exceptions. Three-year-olds will still have frequent and mighty tantrums, but they can also demonstrate good listening skills and emotional responsiveness when gently coached.

# Toddlers Have a Wide Range of Difficult Behavior

Your toddler is learning so much at their age, which is why they *react* to so much at their age. Sometimes their reactions can contain big emotions, push boundaries, and challenge your patience. We're going to discuss some practical strategies to address some common toddler scenarios. I'll also provide some step-by-step cheat sheets to help you approach these issues. Remember to be clear and consistent when correcting behavior; just because something doesn't work on the first try doesn't mean it won't work on the third or fifth or tenth try. Although there are no magic bullets to fix misbehavior, consistently using a mindful parenting strategy will often correct a problem over time.

## Whining

Whining starts when babies first learn to make meaningful sounds. They point toward something and say, "Ehh, ehh," and you immediately try to be responsive by asking, "Oh, you want a bite? You want this toy? You want to be picked up?" You'll jump to accommodate them when they express a need with their primitive language and vague gestures. And so, they learn that whining works. But as their language develops, so should your expectations.

Let's pretend that your toddler begins to whine because he wants a snack.

1. *Be present. Turn to face him, make eye contact, and acknowledge his need: "Hey, sweetie. Thanks for telling me you're hungry."*

2. *Prompt him with a request to express his need in a more socially acceptable way—without whining: "Buddy, if you want a snack, I want you to use your big-boy voice. Please say, 'Mommy, can I have a snack please?'" (Or if they're a young toddler, prompt them with, "Snack, please?")*

3. *If he responds with a version that is at all close to your request, immediately reinforce it:*

   ■ *Verbally acknowledge it: "Yes, sweetheart. I'll get you a snack. Thank you for asking in your big-boy voice."*

   ■ *Get his snack right away. Delaying the snack might cause him to resume whining, and then you'll have to coach him all over again, which will frustrate him and not send the message that he's more likely to get what he wants when he uses his big-boy voice.*

4. *Over time, he'll learn that talking like a big boy gets him what he wants and whining gets him nothing but a prompt to speak at his ability level.*

Reducing or eliminating whining has a huge payoff, as it prevents your toddler from immediately resorting to fretfulness as soon as they have a request. This will support them in regulating their emotions as they expand their vocabulary and learn to communicate in more complex ways.

# Not Listening or Following Instructions

One of the most common frustrations expressed by toddler moms is that their child doesn't listen or follow directions. First of all, toddlers are busy little things. They want to be moving and exploring and asserting their independence, so sometimes Mom's directions are a drag because it just means they have to slow down and prioritize a task that they might not be interested in. There are two questions I ask moms to reflect on first:

1. Are you 100 percent sure that your child knows how to do the task you're asking them to do?

2. If so, are the conditions right for them to display their ability?

   - *Are there few distractions?*

   - *Is your child in a calm state?*

   - *Are the necessary supplies on hand?*

If your little one doesn't know how to do the task, your first job is to teach them. They may need to practice the skill several times before they gain competence, especially if the task requires effort and persistence. If you've seen them exhibit the skill before on multiple occasions, then your role is to motivate them. Sometimes that means encouraging them with praise; other times it means giving a gentle consequence if they disobey.

## Cheat Sheet: Not Listening

Bad listening? Remember these steps:

1.  *Giving the directions in an effective way:*

■ **Proximity:** *Stand or sit close to your toddler as you give the directions.*

■ **Name and eye contact:** *Say their name and make eye contact before giving a direction.*

■ **Simple directions:** *Start with a one-step direction, and tell them what to do instead of what not to do.*

■ **Check for comprehension:** *Ask them to repeat the directions. For example, "What did I say to do? That's right! Put all your blocks in the basket, please."*

■ **Immediate praise:** *Praise them immediately. For example, "Thank you, buddy. You did a great job putting all the blocks away. You're such a good helper."*

■ **Advanced warning of consequences:** *Explain the consequences. You might say, "If you don't clean up all your blocks, we won't be able to go to the park."*

2.  *Immediately and consistently following through with consequences:*

■ *If you make an empty threat and fail to follow through with the stated consequences, your authority will be undermined. Do not make threats you can't enforce, like "no birthday party."*

## How Is Your Childhood Showing Up as a Parent?

All parents make mistakes. It is important to realize that you've experienced the long-term effects (both good and bad) of how you were raised. There are times when new parents default to the parenting behaviors they were raised with ("My parents spanked me, and I'm fine," or "My parents just walked away when I acted badly in the store, and they didn't come back until I was good and sorry"). Maybe that works for you sometimes. But there are other times when you decide to do something better based on your memory of how your parents' behavior made you feel.

The true test of how you are going to parent comes during the stressful moments, like when your child has a tantrum, says hateful words, takes something without asking, or lies.

■ *What is your automatic response?*

■ *Are there certain misbehaviors that feel particularly triggering to you? Why?*

■ *Does the misbehavior feel more personal somehow?*

■ *How did your parents respond when you acted this way?*

■ *How did their response make you feel?*

■ *Is that how you want your child to feel?*

■ *If not, what can you do to prevent this negative interaction between you and your child?*

You can make better choices with your own child, although it may require you to self-examine your default behavior, make a conscious plan to respond differently, and then celebrate when you make progress.

# Saying "No!" and Talking Back

#normal #unpleasant

Society often teaches us that we're not allowed to say no, but it's beneficial to assert control over your own body and set boundaries around your time or activities. But this is different from your toddler saying no to you—their parent.

1. You are their parent, so you have an authority that surpasses that of others.

2. You are asking them to do reasonable things 99.9 percent of the time. Therefore, it's okay to send the message that "When Mommy tells you to do something, you say, 'Yes, Mommy.'" If they don't comply, it may be necessary to give them one extra prompt and then follow through with a consequence, such as ending the activity they're currently enjoying or placing them in a time-out until they're ready to say, "Okay, Mommy." (For more on time-outs, see chapter 4.)

Your first task when your child doesn't follow a direction is to ask yourself these questions:

- *Does my child know how to do the task I'm asking them to do?*

- *Are the conditions adequate for them to display their ability?*

Assuming both of these conditions are met, parents will benefit from remaining calm. It's during these situations when parents are most likely to lose their cool, as it's infuriating to have your child openly defy you.

Modeling self-control is key. Getting defensive and listing all the amazing things you do for them on a regular basis or repeating a version of "I am the parent and you are the child, and you must do what I say" just keeps the power struggle alive and well. Your goal is to end the power struggle with some matter-of-fact directions and an immediate consequence that corresponds to the degree of their disrespect.

## Cheat Sheet: Saying "No!" and Talking Back

1. *Don't be an adult who engages in back talk. Do you respond sarcastically or flippantly to your spouse? Do you say snarky things to the television while watching your favorite show or sports competition? Do you roll your eyes at your mother while you're on the phone? Your child sees that and will imitate it.*

2. *Know the difference between talking back and asking a question. If you tell your child to bring her plate to the sink and she says, "No, you do it," that's different from, "But I still have three more grapes to eat. Can I eat them first?" Leaving no room for asking questions or making observations will take a toll on your parent-child relationship.*

3. *Give them clear feedback and one opportunity to rephrase their response (I call this a "cue and redo"). You might say, "I told you to bring your plate to the sink, please. You need to say, 'Yes, Mommy' and do it right away." If they produce more sass, a time-out is in order. Your child will treat you in the manner you tolerate.*

# Bossiness

Bossiness may be a natural part of a child's personality, so I like to reframe it as "leadership potential" rather than misbehavior. Bossiness in and of itself isn't an issue; it's how their directive nature makes other people feel. If it inspires others to feel excited and motivated to join in, then it should be appreciated. If it's used to shame or invoke fear, then it needs addressing.

## Cheat Sheet: Bossiness

1. *The first step in addressing bossiness is to examine how the adults in your child's life give directions. Is your child imitating your tone or language? Do you refer to yourself as the boss or say things along the line of "because I said so" or "because I want you to"?*

2. *If so, the most effective strategy to alter their manner of expressing a need is to alter your own approach. "Get over here right now" can be shifted to "Come here, please."*

3. *Start teaching your toddler to do these two things:*

■ *Ask others nicely if they want someone to do something.*

■ *Listen and accept the person's response. Did they say, "No, not right now" or "Okay, I will"?*

Your child needs your support to learn to tune in and accept an answer, even if it isn't the one they wanted.

# Telling Tales

Toddlerhood is a child's first foray into telling untruths. Here are some common reasons toddlers tell tales:

1. To express something in their imagination

2. To make a connection (to garner sympathy or praise, for example)

3. To get something ("I only had one candy, and you said I can have two.")

4. To avoid something ("Yes, I already brushed my teeth.")

5. To get out of trouble ("No, I didn't cut my brother's hair.")

It's a normal behavior—frustrating but developmentally appropriate. Being untruthful is not an indicator that your child has a character flaw or isn't developing a conscience. For them, it's simply a means to an end, often done impulsively.

---

### Cheat Sheet: Telling Tales

The best way to respond to your child saying something untruthful is to verbally cue them to the correct, more accurate version. "I can smell peanut butter on your breath, so I know you didn't brush your teeth. Please go do it now. Next time tell me you didn't brush your teeth instead of telling me you did."

---

# Tantrums

Tantrums are a classic component of toddlerhood. They're defined by the child's complete loss of emotional control, consisting of the child crying, screaming, thrashing, lying on the floor, hitting, or wetting themselves. Tantrums vary in length, frequency, and intensity, and they are often instigated by very silly reasons, such as being served dinner on the wrong plate, not being allowed to chew on your car keys, and being forced to leave playdates when they aren't having fun. They're 100 percent normal, 100 percent frustrating, and 110 percent embarrassing when they occur in public. Here are some tips for surviving tantrums:

1. Remember they're typical of this age group.

2. Stay calm so you can ride it out without sinking to their toddler level.

3. Create a plan so you don't respond in an arbitrary manner.

## Cheat Sheet: Tantrums

There are two kinds of tantrums:

1. *A tantrum that consists of a child sitting or lying down, crying or screaming, but not hurting themselves or others*

How to respond: *Leave them alone, withdraw your attention, and serve as a calming force in the background. Discourage others from staring or commenting. Sometimes these tantrums happen in public, and you're forced to shock people with your grace and poise.*

2. *A tantrum that involves kicking, hitting, or biting other people or damaging or attempting to damage property*

How to respond: *Remain calm and guide them to the time-out area quickly (you may have to carry them). Give a simple statement, such as, "You need to go to time-out because you are kicking the wall."*

# Physical Aggression (Hitting, Kicking, and Biting)

Although hitting, kicking, and biting are different behaviors, they stem from the same function or attempt to meet a need. They're physical behaviors that convey anger, a feeling of being overwhelmed, a desire for control, or an attempt to escape something distressing. These moments are usually triggered by a feeling of powerlessness and are exacerbated by fatigue, hunger, worry, or illness.

Physical aggression is an indicator of poor coping, for sure, but your toddler hasn't quite learned how to communicate in a more socially appropriate way. These moments are frustrating, and it can be tempting to surrender to a flash of anger and shout at your toddler, grasp them roughly, or hit back. But it's in these moments that you most need to teach, as your child will learn more from how you act than from what you say.

## Cheat Sheet: Physical Aggression (Hitting, Kicking, and Biting)

1. *Remain calm. You may need to take a deep breath, count backward from 10, or even say aloud, "Mama, stay calm. This is your chance to teach, not react."*

2. *Once you're sure you're calm, proceed by supplying them with a short list of alternative behaviors and providing a consequence, such as a time-out, if they continue using aggression. How you respond sets the stage for how your toddler copes with overwhelming feelings in the future.*

# Acting Out in Public Places

Sometimes kids just have a bad day. They're irritable, they're not feeling equipped to handle the public activity that their mom has planned, or there is a physical or emotional need that hasn't been met and they're trying to let you know. Know that kids don't want to lose their cool in a public place. They're not trying to embarrass you. They're telling you that there is something in that environment they can't handle. In the moment, you're faced with trying to address the need and hope the tantrum passes or abandoning ship and racing to the car.

## Cheat Sheet: Acting Out in Public Places

1. *Use a proactive strategy to elicit positive behavior.*

*Before you leave, present your toddler with two or three clearly stated behavioral expectations and advanced notification of a reward and a consequence. For example, "When we go into the restaurant to eat our lunch, I want you to sit on your bottom, use your spoon, and talk in a quiet voice. If you can't, we will leave, and you will not be able to eat dessert or bring your beverage with you." Be sure to follow through with the consequence or reward.*

2. *Use a reactive strategy to discourage the repetition of misbehavior in public.*

*As you'll learn more about in chapter 4, a time-out (the temporary, quiet removal of a child from the environment in which they misbehaved) can be conducted effectively in public. If your child has not responded to a cue to redo, it may be helpful to use a time-out to reset their behavior before resorting to leaving early.*

# Fighting against Routines

Generally, toddlers gravitate toward routines, especially if it signals that it's uninterrupted time with a loving caregiver. The best routines occur at about the same time every day, proceed in a predictable fashion (consider alternating less-appealing tasks with more-appealing tasks), and provide plenty of opportunity for physical and emotional engagement.

## Bath Time

If your child loves it, then lean in. Build enough time into your evening schedule to allow them to splash away, pausing only to warm the water and wipe up the excess droplets. Never step away from your toddler while they're in the bath, even if you remain within earshot. It's easy for them to slip under the water, turn on the hot water valve, or bump their head. If you must leave the bathroom in a hurry, scoop them up and take them with you. You will get wet, but they will be safe.

### Cheat Sheet: Bath Time

If your child hates the bath, rest assured that this is typically a temporary stage. Proceed with bath time in a cheerful and calm way. Move efficiently, prompting them through each stage. For example, you might say, "I'm going to count to 10, and then your hair will be all washed." Count steadily as you quickly shampoo and rinse their hair. Reassure them with soothing words and a warm towel, then move on to the next activity. If bath time is really distressing, it may be helpful to move it to another time in the day (instead of at bedtime), as it's best to do calming activities right before bed.

# Bedtime

One of the most common mistakes that new toddler moms make is not making bedtime early enough. They think, *I need to wait until they're tired,* and look for signs of fatigue via irritability, eye-rubbing, and a reduced activity level. Instead, you should create bedtime routines that cue your toddler to feel relaxed and sleepy.

## Cheat Sheet: Bedtime

This usually consists of a bath, pajamas, story time (while cuddling), a kiss and hug goodnight, and a calm exit from a darkened room. This routine should occur nightly at the same time and be preserved on weekends and vacations as often as possible.

# Toothbrushing

Toothbrushing is important, but some toddler moms address it with an intensity that far surpasses the need. Kids start out with one or two teeth, and their teeth will be protected by even the most cursory of toothbrushing.

## Cheat Sheet: Toothbrushing

Have them pick out a fun toothbrush, give them a choice of toothpaste flavors, and grin when they noisily spit in the sink. Let them watch you brush your teeth, and raise your expectation of how well they brush as they get more teeth. It's okay to say, "My turn! I'll count to 10," and give a quick countdown as you brush a little more firmly. Remember, if they find toothbrushing at home dramatic, the dentist's office will seem very stressful.

# Refusing to Eat the Food You Serve

This issue can either cause World War III or warrant a shrug and a reminder to yourself that they're healthy and their body will tell them when they're hungry. Although babies often triple their birth weight during infancy, their rate of growth slows dramatically during toddlerhood, and their caloric needs change. Plus, they're busy, busy, busy, and eating can feel like a chore.

When it comes to mealtimes, a parent's role is to provide a variety of healthy foods on a predictable schedule in a reasonably creative manner. In contrast, the toddler's responsibility is to learn to eat what's served, when it's served. However, toddlers don't have the forethought to eat enough now to prevent hunger later, nor do they have the ability to delay gratification and avoid getting distracted to make sure they consume a complete meal. And the reality is, a hungry toddler is an irritable and naughty toddler. The goal is to encourage your child to eat enough at each meal to set them up for success without excessive prompting, bribes, or punishments, which will interfere with your toddler's natural rhythm of eating and cause stress for everyone.

## Cheat Sheet: Refusing to Eat

- *Avoid allowing them to eat while watching TV or using a technological device.*

- *Create a meal that consists of one or two items that have been successfully consumed in the past and add one or two items that are new or have been previously rejected. Toddlers cannot develop a taste for foods that haven't been presented.*

- *Rather than focusing on your child eating, focus on them remaining at the table for an acceptable amount of time. This may be about 15 minutes, as long as they are accompanied by someone who is attending to them in a positive way.*

- *If you decide to prompt them to eat (like setting criteria for what is required before they can have a treat), suggest they take a "polite bite" of each food or eat the number of bites that corresponds to their age (three years old = three bites).*

- *If they do not choose to eat at this meal, try to avoid offering food until the next mealtime.*

- *If you feel they'll be too hungry to wait until the next meal, re-present their leftover food or offer only healthy options (instead of treats or food with high carbs).*

## Refusing to Go to Sleep

Kids don't have to go to sleep. In fact, you can't make them. You can create an environment that is conducive to sleeping. You can teach them coping skills to deal with sleeplessness. You can teach yourself coping skills to deal with the knowledge that your kid may not be resting well that night (and, therefore, may be a monster tomorrow). But you can't *make* anyone fall sleep, especially under pressure.

### Cheat Sheet: Refusing to Go to Sleep

The best way to combat sleep disruption is to establish a bedtime routine, teach them from an early age to sleep in a darkened room (the brain remains alert when there is light), and give them some strategies to cope with those times when falling asleep is difficult. I remember my son was taught to take a sip from his sippy cup, hug his bear, and roll over to face his moon light. He was coached to do those things instead of calling for Mom, getting out of bed, or crying. When he used those coping strategies during the night, he earned a treat in the morning. (I'm pretty sure he still uses a variation of these strategies, and he's much older now.)

## Your Toddler Is Also Experiencing a Lot of "Firsts" That May Require Discipline

Toddlerhood is awash with new experiences. Because discipline is a key component of teaching, there are going to be a lot of opportunities for discipline each time your child experiences a "first." In order to help them adjust, have a brief conversation with your toddler before a new experience and talk about these things:

1. What they can expect to see and do

2. How you expect them to act

3. How you can help them if they are unsure or need help

4. How long you will be there and what you will do to cue them that it's time to leave

Showing kids pictures, videos, or role-playing the event can also help your child adjust to something new and may be essential for the toddler who tends to be more fearful or withdrawn. If the event doesn't go smoothly, it's important for parents to remain calm, consider offering an enticement to encourage the child to attempt something new ("If you open your mouth for the dentist while I count to 20, we can get some ice cream on the way home"), and abandon ship if necessary. Persisting with a new experience that seems extremely stressful to toddlers isn't wise. Instead, step back, do some behind-the-scenes preparation, and retry.

## Going to the Dentist

How you talk about the dentist (or allow others to talk about the dentist in front of your child) can greatly impact their expectations. Usually, children visit the dentist for the first time between the ages of 18 months and 3 years, depending on when they get teeth. Children's dentists are usually fun, brightly colored places that are staffed by smiling professionals who reward good behavior with small toys and treats. It can be fun to play dentist with your child at home (laying them down, peering into their mouth with a small light, tapping their teeth with a finger or a Popsicle stick, and telling them about toothbrushes that have little motors in them that clean teeth really well). If you're a cheerful and calm patient yourself, you may have your little one come with you to your dentist appointment and practice for one to two minutes without the pressure of an actual exam.

## Going on Playdates

Playdates are the best, especially if you get to hang out with another mom you enjoy spending time with. Although you hope that your kids will play together and entertain each other without your involvement, playdates during toddlerhood tend to consist of two types of play:

1. **Parallel play:** Kids play alongside each other but not with each other. For example, both children may be sitting on the floor, but one is playing with blocks and the other is playing with dolls.

2. **Associate play:** Kids do the same activity but with little interaction. For example, both children may be playing in the sandbox or with a train set, but they rarely collaborate or plan together.

Playdates actually get more complicated as toddlers get older and begin interacting more often. They may struggle to share, wait their turn, or use their words to express a need. Toddler playdates will need oversight, as an adult will have to prompt the children to transition between activities and support them in resolving conflicts and managing their emotions.

## A Big-Kid Bed/Their Own Bedroom

What a fantastic milestone! Teaching your child how to sleep independently is a gift that lasts a lifetime. When it's time to tackle this issue, you can start by discussing the transition in a positive way, such as, "I'm so excited that you're going to have a new big-girl bed! You're going to get some good sleep in there." You might pick a particular day to make the official transition, such as on an upcoming weekend, and practice during nap time or quiet time in the days leading up to it. Let them assist as you create a warm and inviting space for them, making sure to bring favorite items from the old space into the new one. Be prepared for some rough moments, as toddlers can struggle with change. We'll discuss more specifics about how to help toddlers adjust to new circumstances in chapter 5.

# Developing Fears

Fears and worries are a natural part of growing up, and they're usually intensified as toddlers seek independence and gain more experience in the larger world. Some common fears include the dark, loud noises, animals, being alone or separated from a parent, getting shots or going to the doctor, or imaginary worries, such as monsters. It can be tempting to strive to eliminate or reduce the fear, as it's difficult to witness your child in distress. However, fears are inevitable, and kids benefit from being sent the message that they are capable of surviving fears with some calming strategies, reassurance, and tolerance of temporary discomfort. Calming strategies that toddlers find most helpful are distraction and truthful statements about the existence of something scary. Giving them "monster spray," for example, would support their mistaken belief that monsters are real; a storybook about how monsters are not real and are simply fearful thoughts would be more productive.

## What's Bothering Your Toddler?

Toddlers, even ones who know a lot of words, are not yet proficient at identifying and expressing their feelings. Therefore, parents may need to investigate to figure out what is bothering their toddler. They can start by asking these questions about their toddler:

- Are they tired, teething, missing a nap, or having more physical activity than usual?
- Are they hungry because they're burning extra calories or going through a growth spurt?
- Are they too cold or too warm?

- Are they experiencing a physical irritant, such as sun in their eyes, a waistband that's pinching them, or a wet diaper or underwear?
- Are they experiencing an emotional irritant, such as boredom, a provoking comment by a parent or peer, or fear (like being in a new place or seeing a barking dog)?

# You Are Not Alone on the Toddler Roller Coaster

Toddlers are adorable and hilarious, but they are also unpredictable. Yesterday, he giggled when you made a funny face; today, he scowled. Yesterday, she tolerated carrots; today, she tossed them on the floor and cried. It's important not to take it personally or evaluate your parenting based on their emotions. Thankfully, there will probably be more awesome days than hard days, especially if you set the stage for success, take care of yourself, and maintain a sense of humor.

The best part of being a toddler mom is the sense of community between toddler moms. They just *get it*. Whether you connect with other moms from your toddler's day care, a neighborhood playgroup, or a local Facebook parenting group, you can always find other parents who are in the same stage of life. Lean on each other. Get tips and encouragement. Share resources. Remember that you're not alone.

# Conclusion

In chapter 3, we discussed some common behavioral challenges faced by toddler parents, as the onset of toddlerhood is typically accompanied by tantrums and power struggles. Although toddlers' quest for exploration and independence is a normal and healthy part of development, it can be challenging for parents to navigate with patience and a sense of confidence. We explored some typical scenarios so you could fill up your parenting toolbox with easily implemented strategies that will set the stage for healthy development and a strong parent-child bond. As we proceed to chapter 4, we'll shift the discussion to some essential characteristics of effective discipline, focusing on the aspects that parents can control.

# The Building Blocks of Toddler Discipline

There are a myriad of strategies that parents can use to support toddlers' behavior and emotional development. In this chapter, you're going to learn the what, how, and why of discipline so you can enhance your parenting ability by establishing yourself as an authority figure, fostering clear and healthy communication, and following through with consistent consequences that will guide your toddler as they learn and grow. This chapter will also prepare you for how to make it through the more harrowing moments while keeping big-picture parenting in the forefront. The recommendations presented here are practical and relatable, with the goal of reminding you that even though toddlerhood has unpredictable moments, there is so much that you can do, Mama, to set the stage for success.

> **"You can't teach children to behave better by making them feel worse. When children feel better, they behave better."**
>
> —Pam Leo

## Mom Moment

During a routine classroom visit, I observed a teacher who did an exceptional job of providing structure, communicating effectively, reinforcing positive behavior, and creating an engaging learning environment. However, the three-year-old girl I was working with was unresponsive. She ignored the teacher and provoked her peers. Upon a follow-up visit to her home, I learned that her parents disciplined her primarily with spanking. They'd give a warning, raise their voice, and then spank. I realized that because the child had rarely been taught a replacement behavior, received reinforcement when well behaved, or been given other consequences (such as time-out or the loss of a privilege), she only responded when she was yelled at or physically disciplined. Her teacher's prompts and gentle coaching were overlooked. Because the teacher wasn't going to get physical or shout, it wasn't even on the child's radar to listen. Within a few weeks, Mom and Dad had eliminated the spanking and developed a parenting toolbox full of strategies to teach, reinforce, and provide nonphysical consequences, and their little girl was well on her way to being a positive addition to the classroom setting. Everyone breathed a sigh of relief, as home life and school life had become much calmer.

# What Is Discipline?

According to the American Academy of Pediatrics, *discipline* refers to the process of teaching and nurturing children. The purpose of discipline is to aid children in developing a sense of self-worth, self-control, self-direction, and empathy toward others. In order for discipline to be effective, the following elements must be in place:

- *A positive and supportive parent-child relationship*
- *A proactive strategy to teach and reinforce positive behavior*
- *A reactive strategy to decrease or eliminate misbehavior*

Discipline also tends to be more successful when parents have a clear understanding of what behavior their child is capable of at each developmental stage. It's hard to know what behavior to encourage or discourage when you're not confident of how to set age-appropriate expectations.

# Why Do We Need to Discipline Our Toddlers?

All children need discipline; they need to be taught and nurtured. Although toddlers are inquisitive and naturally seek stimulation, attention, and affection, adults are responsible for guiding them toward behavior that is most compatible with their environment and away from behavior that would be detrimental to themselves or others. (Adults are also responsible for making the environment compatible with their toddler.) Toddlers are smart, curious, and strive to gain autonomy, but their brains aren't fully developed, nor do they have the breadth of experience of older kids and adults. They naturally gravitate toward stimulating activities that make them feel good. However, they don't have the foresight to consider what could happen if something goes awry.

## Create Safe Parameters for Your Child

I was once asked to go over to a friend's house and walk their dog in the evening. With me was my three-and-a-half-year-old son and his same-age peer. As we were walking along with the elderly dog, I noticed a car was creeping along the street, moving at the same slow pace as we were. I said to my son and his friend, "Boys, we need to go inside right now. Those people are strangers, and I don't know why they are so close to us. We need to go inside right now to be safe." My son responded to the urgency in my tone, began hurrying, and was alert and responsive to my directions. His friend, known to be less responsive to adult directions, whined, "Why do we have to go inside, Ms. Tara? I want to stay on our walk," and he failed to pick up his pace. I heard a male voice from the car say something to me and the other men laugh. In a flash, I grasped the back of my son's friend's shirt and began pulling him briskly, ordering, "I need you to listen right now and come inside to be safe." Shocked at my harsh tone and physical touch, he stopped protesting, and we got inside and locked the door. I called my son's friend's parents and explained what had happened, as I did not want my physical handling of their son to be misunderstood. Thankfully, they trusted my judgment and were grateful that I had gotten their son to safety so quickly.

Although this is an extreme example of why it's important for your child to respond appropriately to your directives, it illustrates the frustration that can occur from children failing to comply. Thankfully, the majority of daily tasks are routine in nature and have pretty low stakes. However, getting in a power struggle with your child after giving a clearly stated directive can indicate that your child may not view you as an authority figure and they may feel prompts are negotiable or only to be followed if Mom loses her cool or places them in a significantly uncomfortable situation.

## Establish Family Rules

In chapter 2, we discussed how moms usually set the tone in the home. This applies to both the emotional tone and the family rules and routines. Toddlers are better listeners when rules and routines are clearly stated, consistently modeled, and immediately reinforced. Toddlers are most likely to comprehend two or three simple household rules.

Here are some examples of helpful family rules:

1. Use gentle hands and feet. (No hitting or kicking. Touch each other and the dog softly.)

2. Say please and thank you.

3. Be a good listener. (When Mommy or Daddy asks you to do something, say yes.)

When children follow these rules, it's important that parents use specific praise, such as, "Jesse, you have such wonderful manners! Thank you for saying 'please' when I poured you some milk."

## Lay the Foundation for Healthy Long-Term Habits

I often tell my clients, "Don't let your child do something today that you don't want them to do tomorrow." For example, don't let your toddler jump on the couch, sleep in your bed, talk back, or use your things without asking if you don't want them to make a habit of it. Even if toddlers are still a little too young to understand the nuances of your reasoning, it's still important to lay the groundwork for what's acceptable and unacceptable.

## Maintain Your Sanity

It takes so much more energy to be stressed and angry than it does to be calm and cheerful. So, if you're caring for your toddler day in, day out, and you feel like all you're doing is yelling and punishing them, then understand that this dynamic is not sustainable. It's too stressful. Your child has a long childhood in front of them, and the goal is for you both to enjoy it, *most* of the time. In order to do this, you'll need to establish a strong parent-child bond, create some healthy routines, and provide clear consequences for those times when your child is struggling to adhere to well-established, developmentally appropriate behavioral expectations.

### The Difference between Discipline and Punishment

Remember, discipline is a process of teaching and nurturing. It focuses on a strong parent-child bond *and* proactive strategies that set the stage for behavioral success. The third and final component—a reactive strategy to eliminate or decrease misbehavior—is where the concept of punishment is introduced. The term *punishment* often conjures harsh images of yelling or spanking. Although those are, indeed, punishments, the true definition of punishment is simply the process of adding something unpleasant to the environment (insisting your child clean up the mess they made) or taking away something desirable (like dessert) after your child misbehaves to decrease the likelihood of them misbehaving again. Some kids benefit from experiencing this kind of punishment after a misbehavior occurs, as it reminds them it would be best to make a different choice the next time they're faced with the same opportunity to misbehave.

# How Is Toddler Discipline Unique?

Once your child hits toddlerhood, you shift from simply being responsive to your child to asserting limits. It's a first-time behavior for both mother and toddler, and it can take time for you to learn where your boundaries need to be firm and where flexibility is helpful. Similarly, your toddler is learning when *no* means no and when *no* means "wait until Mom is on the phone or it's time for bed and she's too tired to argue."

## They Are Curious and Adventurous

Toddlers learn by doing. They play, explore, and test limits, and they'll nearly always look over their shoulder to see your response. Responding with enthusiasm and encouragement when they try new things will foster confidence, resiliency, and curiosity. These characteristics will serve them well, particularly as they grow and learn to temper their impulses and plan ahead.

## They Are Pushing Boundaries

Toddlers are impulsive and love to interact with their environment. There are times when they'll just barrel ahead, with little regard for rules or potential consequences. Other times, you'll see them give you the side-eye as they willfully disregard your boundaries. This is natural, although it speaks to the need for a consistent response and good supervision.

## They Are Learning to Communicate

Between the ages of one and two, toddlers have a burst of language development, and with it come the questions. Oh, the endless questions! "Why, Mommy, why?" Sometimes it seems like they're all talk and no listen, but make no mistake, they are absorbing what you say and do. Watch your toddler carefully, and tune in to their words, their body language, their facial expressions, and their gestures. Chances are, you'll recognize something of yourself in them, for better or worse.

# Short-Term Parenting and Long-Term Parenting

Two terms I teach my clients are *short-term parenting* and *long-term parenting*. Short-term parenting is the parenting you do in the moment, designed to get you through a specific event or day. It's the type of parenting that keeps everyone safe and happy-ish, but it doesn't really reinforce the big-picture goals you have for your child. Certain days are rougher than others, and sometimes you're not equipped to be Super Mom. On those days, you just need to power through until bedtime. Here are some examples of short-term parenting:

- *Allowing your child to have an extra cupcake at Grandma's birthday party to avoid a tantrum*

- *Letting them watch toddler-friendly videos on your phone while you're sitting in traffic for an hour*

- *Saying nothing as you watch your son pee on the floor while you're on a work call with your boss*

- *Allowing them to crawl into bed with you in the middle of the night because you're just too tired to walk them back to their room*

Long-term parenting, in contrast, is when you tolerate short-term discomfort so you can meet a big-picture goal. You may be trying to extinguish a misbehavior or start the process of teaching your toddler a new skill that will result in more independence. These moments are typically more laborious and frustrating, but it's more about the long game. Here are some examples of long-term parenting:

- *Staying close to home for a week so you can be extra responsive to your toddler as they're being potty trained*

- *Listening to your toddler "cry it out" each night as you implement a plan to teach them to sleep the entire night in their own bed*

- *Strictly limiting their TV time to 45 minutes per day and being extra engaging as you teach them how to find other ways to entertain themselves*

Generally, it's good to remain in long-term parenting mode as much as possible, as a consistent and mindful parenting strategy that encourages prosocial behavior and discourages misbehavior is going to pay off in the long term with a well-behaved, more independent toddler. However, sometimes you just need to give them a cookie so you can have a phone conversation or enjoy a snack of your own.

## Make a Plan

One of the defining characteristics of short-term parenting is that you don't have a plan. You're just making it through. However, long-term parenting is most likely to be successful when you have a plan. Having a plan lends itself to more effective communication with your toddler, more consistency and patience, and a greater sense of competence for both parent and child when there's a win. These long-term parenting goals, for example, require a plan:

- *Establishing a smooth morning routine*

- *Creating a relaxing bedtime routine*

- *Transitioning from one activity to another*

- *Responding calmly and consistently to temper tantrums*

Having a plan prevents you from responding impulsively in the moment, second-guessing yourself, or giving in to your toddler and then regretting it later.

# First Things First: You've Got This

Take a deep breath, Mama. You are the queen of your castle, much beloved by your little one. Raising a toddler is hard, for sure, but you are the best mom for your child. Tantrums will be

outgrown, potty training will be mastered, and their comprehension will continue to develop until they one day chortle at a
sex joke overheard on the television. Generally, kids get better as
they age (yes, even teenagers), especially if you've created a relationship that's mutually respectful, establishes your authority,
and has plenty of lighthearted moments.

## Stay Calm

No one calms down by being told to calm down, am I right?
(Ask my husband how he knows this.) We know that becoming
emotionally escalated causes more chaos, not less, especially if
it causes our child to feel fearful or ashamed. In my most fraz-
zled moments, I've been known to continuously murmur, "No
one calms down by being yelled at." As we've already mentioned,
moms usually set the tone in the home. Fair or not, everyone is
likely to look to you as they're deciding how to respond to a given
event. If you're losing your cool, so will everyone else.

However . . .

### It's Okay If You Get Upset! You're Human, Not a Robot

Parents who haven't yelled at their kids are like unicorns.
They don't exist. Even the most laid-back mom will lose her
patience occasionally.

But keep these things in mind:

- *Don't yell all the time because your child will start treating
  your yelling voice like it's your normal voice, and you will
  need to stay in a constant state of stress just to feel heard.*

- *Don't use words that are harsh or hateful. There is a big difference between "Look at this mess! Come over here and clean this up!" and "I can't stand you anymore!" or "You are such a pig!"*

- *Your raised voice should not cause your child to feel ashamed or like you've withdrawn your love.*

Side note: How you talk to your kid sets the tone for how they speak to you, their siblings, and themselves.

## Empathize with What Your Toddler Is Going Through

One of the best ways to teach empathy is to model how to validate feelings. Validating feelings doesn't mean that you need to agree that the child's feelings are rational; it simply means that you recognize their feelings and honor them. When your toddler doesn't want to get out of the pool, for example, you might say, "Oh, I know, honey. It's really disappointing to have to get out of the pool when you're having so much fun swimming." Toddlers really benefit from adults helping them name their feelings. Once the feelings are named and recognized, you can encourage your toddler to use a coping strategy to move past them. For instance, for the pool example, you could say, "I know you're frustrated that it's time to go. Do one more big jump into the pool, and then we'll dry off. Ready, set, go!"

# Communicate Clearly

One of the biggest missteps parents make is to talk, talk, talk. When a toddler mom uses 657 words to state a basic direction, possibly using a nagging or lecturing tone, toddlers just tune out. Of those 657 words, they're not sure which ones to focus on, so they may decide to focus on none. Instead, state your expectation with toddler-friendly words in an upbeat tone. Don't present your direction as a question unless you're actually giving them a choice. Instead of "How about we go put your shoes on?" try "Let's go put your shoes on, sweetie. It's time to go to swimming lessons."

Another misstep parents make is sending mixed messages. You might tell your toddler, "Look at Mommy when you're talking to her," but then keep your face buried in your cell phone. You might say, "Use kind words," but then yell at the dog. When you're speaking to your toddler, reflect on your tone, your words, your facial expressions, and the gestures you use. They should send a cohesive message as often as possible.

## Spanking Is a Big No

Spanking is physical punishment that typically involves hitting a child with an open hand, typically across the buttocks. The intent is to cause physical pain or discomfort in order to modify the child's behavior. Spanking is a power assertion technique that is used in lieu of reasoning, emotional coaching, or setting firm limits with nonaggressive consequences (such as time-out).

## What does spanking do?

- Gets kids' attention
- Usually results in an immediate cessation of behavior
- Causes physical pain
- Inspires fear, confusion, or embarrassment
- Models physical aggression as a problem-solving strategy
- Causes an escalation in distress during the incident
- Leads to long-term psychological distress (anxiety, trust issues, depression) and increased behavioral problems
- Causes kids to focus on their victimhood instead of taking responsibility for their choices
- Reduces their responsiveness to nonviolent forms of punishment
- Erodes the parent-child relationship

## What does spanking NOT do?

- Teach kids what they *should* do instead of what they *should not* do
- Result in long-term change
- Model appropriate self-restraint or emotional regulation
- Cause them to respect the adult who is using corporal punishment
- Increase conflict-resolution skills, communication skills, or critical-thinking skills

Spanking results in a child learning that when people get mad, they hit, which means that when they get mad, they're more likely to hit, too.

# Expanding Your Toddler-Mom Toolbox to Include Time-Out

Toddlers can be crafty, especially when they're determined to persist with a behavior that is not toddler mom–approved. As already stated, it is strongly recommended that parents refrain from using spanking as a punishment for misbehavior, as research indicates that spanking does not result in long-term behavior change. It inspires fear, and it erodes the parent-child relationship. So, what tool should parents use when their toddler exhibits behavior that is simply unacceptable?

Time-out is the preferred method. Time-out is the temporary, quiet removal of a child from the environment in which they misbehaved. It is an effective way to send a stubborn toddler the message to stop doing what they're doing without getting into a lengthy power struggle or losing your cool when they disregard your directions, show aggression, or persist with a dangerous or disruptive behavior.

However, using time-out effectively requires more than sitting your child in the corner for two minutes. Time-out, when applied consistently and immediately following the misbehavior, sends your child these messages:

1.  Fun and/or reinforcement stops when misbehavior starts.

2.  The daily routine will not continue until they are calm and responsive to basic directions.

3.  You will let them know immediately if they've made a poor choice, and you will tell them so in a calm and clear way.

4.  You will decide when time-out begins and when time-out ends.

5. You will always work to teach them how to make a better choice next time.

6. They are a competent, smart child who, with practice, can learn to control themselves and make good choices.

Before proceeding with the remainder of this chapter, let's discuss how to effectively use time-out as a discipline strategy.

## The Right Way to Use Time-Out

For time-out to be most effective, you must teach your child how to do time-out. This means parents and caregivers need to be on the same page with regard to how time-out will be implemented, the child needs to be given a brief description about what to expect during time-out (and ideally, practice via role-play beforehand), and the parents need to follow through each and every time their toddler displays a behavior worthy of time-out.

When choosing the location of a time-out, keep these things in mind:

- *It should be safe.*

- *It should be boring. (Remember, the goal is to withdraw all reinforcement.)*

- *It should be within sight of the parent, especially if the child is a younger toddler, or within earshot to prevent fear or feelings of abandonment.*

One of the most challenging aspects for toddler moms is getting their toddler to remain in time-out. For example, if a mother sets their child on the bottom stair step, the toddler will usually rise and follow Mom as she steps away. For little ones, it's important to choose a time-out location the child cannot leave: for example, a high chair, a Pack 'n Play, or even an unused car seat with the buckles gently fastened. It is not recommended that parents physically hold their child to keep them in time-out, for the following reasons:

- *It typically leads to aggression from the child because they'll struggle to escape.*

- *The child is still engaging with the parent, which reinforces misbehavior.*

- *Parents are less likely to remain calm and disengaged, as they're unable to step away from their child and hit the reset button on their patience.*

Once the location is determined and the child is placed in time-out, the parent should completely disengage from the child, even if the child is crying, screaming, or kicking. Often parents are tempted to keep up a running stream of commentary ("Don't pull the dog's tail. It hurts him and then he might bite you. I've told you over and over again.") or offer well-meaning prompts ("Calm down so you can come finish your lunch. Mommy loves you, and she wants you to snuggle with her on the couch later.") Sometimes this line of communication evolves into cajoling, bribing, or pleading, such as, "Please, buddy. Take a deep breath. If you stop crying, I'll get you a Popsicle."

If your toddler is new to time-out or struggles to calm themselves after several minutes (gasping or at-risk of vomiting), you can sit quietly near them and model taking exaggerated deep breaths, repeating a soothing phrase, such as, "Calm down. Take deep breaths, like this." Parents should avoid eye contact or other conversation and just serve as a reassuring presence and a role model for using a calming strategy. The goal isn't to calm them down; it's to help them learn to calm themselves down.

# How Do You Know When Time-Out Is Over?

When the child is calm enough to respond to adult directives, time-out can end. If they're still tearful, that's fine. For example, if you ask, "Are you ready to come out and show me that you can pet the dog nicely?" they should be able to nod and respond to the question. If they just screech back or swat at you, they're not ready. Allowing toddlers to come out of time-out while they're in the middle of a temper outburst sends the message that if you scream long enough, Mom will get you out of time-out. That is not a good message for your toddler to receive. Instead, listen carefully to your child, and once they're calm, you can immediately reinforce it:

- *Praise their ability to calm down (even if it took a while).*

- *Remind them why they were put in time-out. ("You are in time-out because you pulled the dog's tail and you hurt him.")*

- *Tell them what they can do next time. ("Next time, pet the dog with an open hand, like this, and tell Mommy if he's bothering you.")*

- *Transition to the next activity with a positive attitude. ("All right, let's go pet the dog in a nice way and then go finish our lunch.")*

## Appropriate Age to Use Time-Out

Developmentally, most toddlers aren't able to understand the purpose of time-out until they're between 18 and 24 months old. Because their memories are so short, toddlers younger than 18 months will not understand the relationship between a misbehavior and setting them in a quiet location; it will just seem confusing. So, what can you do if your child misbehaves but they are too young to place in time-out?

1. Say no in a firm way, followed by a simple two- or three-word phrase that describes the misbehavior. For example, "No, Lauren, no hitting. That hurts."

2. Then remove your toddler from the situation and redirect them to something else. For example, if your daughter pulled the dog's tail, tell her, "No, Lauren. Do not pull the dog's tail." Then pick her up and move her to a different location to play with something else. This accomplishes two things:

   ■ *Removing the temptation of repeating the misbehavior*

   ■ *Redirecting the child's attention to an activity that is more acceptable*

## What about Time-Out in Public?

Time-out can be used when you're away from home, particularly once your toddler is well-versed in the time-out process and knows not to leave the time-out area. At this point, your toddler should understand that the quickest way to get back to fun activities is to hit the reset button. If you are away from home, your car can always be a time-out spot, as your toddler can be placed in their car seat and the parent can sit quietly in the car or stand outside in the child's line of sight. If you're at a friend's house or in a store, you can designate a time-out spot (such as in the shopping cart) and direct them to that spot if necessary. It's not ideal, but it may prevent you from having to leave your event prematurely.

## Provide Verbal Guidance . . . and Repeat

Toddler moms will often sigh in exasperation and say, "I've said this over and over." Yup. You will. Toddlers have short memories and act on impulse, so they're always tempted to do the thing that feels good rather than the thing you said. So, create two to three rules that are age-appropriate, repeat them verbally, draw a picture for each rule, and post them so they can be easily referenced. Most important, reinforce your child when they follow these rules. Times 100. It's slow going, but consistency will win.

## Don't Make Empty Threats

Recently, I heard a mom tell her son that if he didn't pick up the toys left on the floor, she was going to cancel his birthday party. Spoiler alert: She wasn't going to cancel her three-year-old's birthday party because some blocks were left on the floor. It was an empty threat—a threat she would never follow through on. Your child will quickly learn when you're full of poo, and too many instances of this will undermine your authority. Instead, give consequences that match the severity of the misbehavior, hold fast and firm, and give a simple explanation of your reasoning.

## Establish Guidelines/Boundaries

Know your limits, Mama. It will help keep you sane. For example, I knew from the time my oldest child was three days old that I was not equipped to sleep with a kid in my bed. It was an adult-only space with the magical power to create a mommy who was reasonably well-rested and patient day after day. Other moms have boundaries about kids eating their food, climbing on them without an invitation, interrupting their workday when at home with the nanny . . . the list goes on and on. Think about what your boundaries are and respect them. Doing so will model for kiddos how to establish their own limits as they get older.

## Be Consistent

The opposite of consistent is arbitrary. When I work with kids who struggle to meet their parents' expectations, it's typically because they feel their parents' rules have no rhyme or reason. For example: "Sometimes Mom lets me sleep in her bed. Other times it makes her mad," or "Sometimes Mom acts silly when I make gross noises at the table. Other times I'm in trouble, and I get yelled at." Toddlers look to you to cue them as to what is acceptable or unacceptable behavior, and if you're inconsistent, they feel frustrated and helpless.

## Do Your Best to Remain in Control

The best way to remain in control is to determine what you actually have control of and focus on controlling that. For example, you do not have control over whether your child actually picks up the food you prepared, puts it in their mouth, and swallows it (you're not going to force-feed them, obviously). You do, however, have control over the type of food you prepare, how and when it's presented, and your response should it not get eaten. Will you prepare a different meal if they don't eat this one? (No.) Will you yell at them? (Also no.) Will you refrain from offering food until the next mealtime? (Yes.)

When you spend a lot of time trying to control things that you cannot control, it just leads to a power struggle that a stubborn toddler is likely to win. So, avoid that scenario and ask yourself, *What can I control in this situation?*

## Model Good Behavior

You're not perfect, Mama. You're going to eat standing over the sink, use bad words sometimes, and lose your temper. Your toddler is going to see you do this. But you can also make sure you show them how you calm yourself when stressed, how to apologize and make amends, and how to turn a tense moment into something funny. Modeling how to make a better decision after making a poor decision is just as important as consistently making good decisions. Remember, your toddler isn't the only one learning, and no one is perfect.

A fun exercise to do with your child is to role-play. You might tell them, "You be me—Mommy. I'll be you—Olivia. Let's pretend that it's time to put Olivia to bed. You're the mommy. I'm Olivia. Show me how we should go to bed." You can role-play your child as if they're doing everything the correct way (even if it's not the most truthful account), or you can show a feistier version and see how your child-as-mommy reacts. You can then switch roles, using it as an opportunity to teach and reinforce. At bedtime, you'll be able to say, "Remember what we practiced? You can do it, sweetie!"

# Distractions: The Good and the Bad

Toddlerhood is the perfect age to use distractions. Their memory is short, their interest in visual stimuli is high, and many, many tantrums will be thwarted with the generous use of "Look at that! Do you see it?" Maybe you're veering away from the ice cream truck, drawing their attention away from a toy their peer is holding, or distracting them from focusing on the boo-boo on their knee. Word of caution: Don't distract them by capitulating on a rule or boundary that's been established beforehand. For example, you wouldn't want to distract them from their boo-boo by letting them eat seven cookies for lunch or let them jump on the bed because they mentioned missing Daddy because he's late coming home from work. Distract them with silly games, pointing out that the garbage truck is going by, or calling Grandma on video chat.

# When to Ignore Your Toddler's Behavior

Ignoring an undesirable misbehavior can be an excellent way of extinguishing it. If you don't provide attention as a result of a specific behavior, you won't reinforce the behavior, and it will just fade away. This is tough to do if you're not a patient person, as it can be tempting to scold, sigh in exasperation, or get fed up and apply punishment. Some examples of behavior that might be helpful to ignore, if you truly have the self-restraint, are whining (like when you're in the car), random self-stimulating noises, silliness (such as saying bathroom words), calling out to you when they're in time-out, or crying when you leave their bedroom at night.

# How to Approach Praise

When it comes to praise, keep it short, sweet, and specific. For example, "Mama, you're doing great reading this book. You're learning so much. I appreciate your reading it and passing it on to a friend." See what I did there? I used your name, told you exactly what I appreciated, and kept it brief and sincere.

# Let Your Toddler Have Some Independence

Maria Montessori, an Italian physician and educator, once said, "Never help a child with a task at which he feels he can succeed." While I don't agree with this 100 percent (sometimes you do things for your child simply because it makes them feel cherished), I understand the sentiment. You feel proud of yourself when you try new things and succeed, even if you fail a few times first. This is the reality and benefit of learning via trial and error. Toddlerhood is the first time that children exert autonomy, and it's essential that you supervise rather than hover, and teach rather than correct. They will learn as they go, and they will be thrilled when you are nearby to witness their success.

# Set Yourself and Your Toddler Up for Success

You know what to do and when to do it. All you need is to follow through. That can be the toughest part, particularly during one of those days that seems to last 32 hours instead of 24. That is when having a strong support system comes in handy. A pep talk from a friend or family member or getting a babysitter so you can have some adult time followed by a good night's sleep can make all the difference. Taking care of yourself is essential, as you'll need to muster your stamina to persist through the tantrums and reinforce the rules.

## Conclusion

In chapter 4, we discussed discipline: what it is, why it's important, and how toddler moms can implement it with integrity while staying sane. Some highlights included the perils of spanking, the benefits of using an effective time-out strategy, and some general information about how to set the stage for success and give consequences, as necessary. As we proceed to chapter 5, the focus will shift to answering some of the most common questions posed by toddler moms.

# Toddlers in the Real World

You've made it to the final chapter, Mama! Hopefully, your parenting toolbox is now chock-full of helpful recommendations to address the myriad challenges that toddlerhood involves. In this final chapter, I've assembled a few of the most common toddler-mom questions and provided a detailed response to each. Each scenario is genuine, relatable, and emphasizes that your experience is probably not so different from that of other moms.

"Don't let yourself become so concerned with raising a good kid that you forget that you already have one."

—Glennon Doyle

# Questions and Answers

As a clinician, answering parents' questions is a huge component of my job. This chapter includes some of the questions I get asked the most with answers that incorporate the tools you've learned throughout this book.

**Q:** *My toddler throws a tantrum every time we go to the grocery store. He grabs items off the shelves, screams at the top of his lungs, and tries to kick me when I calmly tell him no. I don't have any help at home, so I have to take him with me. What can I do?*

My response involves five components:

1. **Give advanced warning:** Tell your little guy what behavior you expect from him when you arrive at the store. Keep it simple, two or three directions max, like, "You need to sit in the shopping cart, use a quiet voice, and eat your snack."

2. **Describe the consequence:** "If you don't sit in the shopping cart, use a quiet voice, and eat your snack, then we will leave the store right away, and we will not (*insert fun thing, like stopping at the park or getting a treat*)."

3. **Distract:** Bring something for your toddler to do while you're walking around the store. This might be a snack cup of crackers that take a long time to eat, or you can chat with him cheerfully the entire time and have him hold favorite purchases (that aren't breakable) as you take them off the shelves.

4. **Be realistic:** Toddlers aren't going to remain well behaved if you take them on a massive, two-hour shopping

trip. Set them up for success by making the trip shorter, arriving with a specific list, and giving a clear description of how long you plan to stay.

5. **Timing:** Don't go to the store when your toddler is hungry or tired. Try to go right before an appealing activity, such as a playdate with a friend or a stop at the library. Remind him of the fun activity coming up, and make a show of going efficiently through the store so you can get to the fun activity. Be prepared to cancel the fun activity should his behavior warrant it.

6. **Follow through:** Be sure to give the stated consequence or reward.

*Q: I found out that my mother-in-law is not following the guidelines we set for how to discipline our toddler when she is babysitting him. In fact, she does the exact opposite of what we have discussed. I want to be respectful of her and her relationship with my child, but the mixed messaging is very confusing for him.*

Once you leave your child in your mother-in-law's care, you really don't have control over whether she complies with your guidelines. Assuming you've expressed your preferences clearly and consistently, your choices are limited.

1. Allow your mother-in-law to make the decisions when she is supervising but uphold your standards when your toddler is in your care. If he's a quick learner and a people pleaser, he will learn to adjust his behavior to correspond to his caregiver's expectations. If he's a bit more strong-willed, this probably isn't going to be an effective strategy.

2. Give your mother-in-law a clear and calm warning, and then if she doesn't respect your boundaries, find another childcare option. It would probably be best for your spouse to set this boundary with his mother, not you.

3. Find another childcare option.

If you decide to seek a different childcare provider, do so in the spirit of minimizing strife and resentment and maintaining a positive relationship with your mother-in-law rather than punishing her for not caring for your toddler in the manner you prefer. You're all adults and can make your own decisions. In this instance, you might decide "my child, my way" and choose to have your child connect with his grandmother in more of a "fun grandma" kind of way instead of as a childcare provider.

**Q: My daughter is two years old, and I'm planning to go back to work full-time in a couple of weeks. We're enrolling her in a great full-time childcare program. How can I help her adjust to the new day care?**

Returning to work is stressful enough, but it's made even worse by separating from your adorable toddler. If your schedule allows it, start by bringing her on a school visit, showing her around the classroom, introducing her to her teachers, and allowing her to visit the playground. Remind her that this is her new school, where she will play and make new friends. Include her in choosing a new backpack and water bottle and packing extra clothes, and supply her with a familiar lovey from home and a laminated picture of your family that she can keep in her pocket or backpack. Before dropping her off at school for the first time, tell her exactly what to expect with regard to your goodbyes. Tell her, "I'm going to bring you into your class, help you hang up your coat, and then we're going to say good morning to your teacher.

I will give you two kisses and a hug, and then I will say goodbye and see you after nap time." Don't linger in the class, Mama, and try not to get emotional until you get to the car. If you're concerned about your little one crying or missing you, call the school and have someone peek into her class to reassure you that she's calm and enjoying her day.

**Q: *My son just turned three years old, and he's the only child among my friends' kids who's not potty trained. He just doesn't seem interested in learning and sometimes throws tantrums when we tell him to use the potty. What should we do?***

Take a break. Potty training seems to be causing him stress rather than giving him a sense of competence and pride. Put him back in diapers and only prompt him to use the potty when he's changing clothes (such as when he undresses to get in the bath or when he wakes up and is getting dressed). Wait three to six weeks, then try again, using a reward that is only permitted when he's on the potty. For example, some parents will deny their child an opportunity to use an iPad unless they're sitting on the potty, or they will only allow access to a coveted treat if their child has urinated in the potty.

For some toddlers, potty training is relatively drama-free, and they're able to demonstrate mastery within a couple of weeks. Other toddlers really struggle, for reasons like these:

1. Underdeveloped bladder: They may not be able to hold urine produced during the night.

2. Inability to sense a full bladder

3. Chronic constipation: The same muscles control urine and stool elimination, and long-term constipation can

impact these muscles and impair the child's ability to stay dry all night.

4. Health concerns such as a hormonal imbalance, a urinary tract infection, or sleep apnea

In order for a toddler to potty train, they need to be interested enough to persist with something that requires a change in their behavior. Here are some things you can do to set your child up for success:

- **Avoid starting too young.** *You can wait until they're developmentally ready and spend three weeks potty training, or you can start six months earlier and spend six months and three weeks potty training. The latter causes more frustration for both of you and is likely to instigate several bouts of regression.*

- **Stay low-key.** *Gently expose them to the potty by way of positive talk, no pressure. Allow them to see you use the potty, get them their own toddler-size potty, and admire the big-kid underwear in the store (and maybe purchase some if they're interested).*

- **Give them a chance.** *Let them try out the potty when they're transitioning between getting dressed and undressed and before they get in the bath (it can't hurt to leave the water running to inspire some tinkles). Should they successfully urinate, give an enthusiastic response like clapping or bragging about it to another family member.*

- **Reinforce.** *Initially, parents should reinforce all attempts to produce urine while sitting on the potty. Once your toddler has shown the ability to willfully urinate in the potty, parents should reinforce them each time they successfully* *urinate in the potty (my son was a big fan of receiving five gummy candies for peeing in the potty). Then encourage them to poop in the potty.*

**Q: *My toddler is often clingy. She cries if I ask her to do something independently and rarely wants to try something new. She is more timid around me than around my husband. What can I do to encourage her to be more independent?***

This is a tough one, as it can be difficult to walk the line between making her feel secure and nurtured and inadvertently encouraging her to be overly dependent. In fact, kids with more timid personalities can be undermined by parents who don't gently expand their world, as they will develop a self-perception that they are less competent than others.

One of the most effective ways to deal with fear of a new situation is to be exposed to it gently at first and gradually increase the intensity of the exposures over time. First, you might read books with your toddler about a new activity. You might show her pictures or videos on YouTube (preview them first!) or have her watch you try the new activity. Allow her to go at her own pace, with little pressure from you. Letting another adult supervise instead might help her avoid defaulting to her typical clingy behavior and get past her initial reluctance. Reward all attempts, and it's okay to motivate her with a reward that she can have *immediately* following a successful attempt.

**Q: *How can I encourage my toddler to behave appropriately in a restaurant?***

First of all, avoid taking a toddler to a restaurant that is not kid friendly. It sets your toddler up for failure, causes you stress due to unrealistic behavioral expectations, and results in the other patrons giving you dirty looks. It's no fun for anyone. Instead, choose a kid-friendly restaurant, feed them something before you go if they're too hungry to wait (maybe some cereal from the snack cup in the diaper bag), give them something to do with their hands (such as eating bits of bread, coloring, or playing with a toy), and give them positive attention while they're behaving.

Word of advice: Parents are often tempted to let their toddlers get down from their seat because they're bored, but this sets a precedent for them to wander around a restaurant instead of learning to use what's within arm's reach to entertain themselves. If your toddler is too wiggly or upset to remain at the table, have an adult walk around with them outside or just pack up your leftovers and go.

**Q: *Is there ever a time when bribery should be used to convince my toddler to do something she doesn't want to do?***

For sure. I encourage parents to use bribery if the task is a low-frequency, high-stress event, such as going to the pediatrician. I never advise it for a routine task like running into the grocery store for a few items when the child is well-rested and fed. Bribery should only be used occasionally. Otherwise, children will just begin to feel entitled to a particular treat, and its power will be diminished. Sometimes you know you're pushing your luck and asking your toddler to do something beyond what is expected for their developmental stage. This is when presenting something amazing might come in handy.

Here are some examples:

- *Giving them some small candies one at a time while you're in line at the DMV.*

- *Allowing them to pick out a small toy after a successful visit to the dentist.*

- *Presenting them with a doughnut after they've slept in their bed all night.*

We all like to be appreciated after a job well done.

**Q: *We're expecting baby number two in three months. What can we do to prepare our toddler for a new sibling?***

Congratulations on your upcoming addition! Although the first few weeks following the arrival of new baby can be pretty eventful as everyone in the house adjusts, toddlers usually love becoming a big sibling. In the weeks leading up to the birth, toddlers benefit from parents educating them on what to expect from a newborn. Some highlights to mention: they will not be able to play with your toddler, they cry, they poop a lot, and they will live with your family forever. Parents can share information via books, YouTube videos, or visits with friends or family with a newborn. Toddlers can be included in conversations about preparing a nursery for the baby, and they can help Mom pick out new clothes or toys. Keep in mind that the baby is going to seem like an abstract concept until he/she actually arrives and gets settled into the home.

Once the baby arrives, toddlers love to help in age-appropriate ways, like fetching a diaper, gently holding the baby while sitting on the couch with parental supervision, or singing to the baby. Although friends and family members will be tempted to marvel over the new baby's cuteness, they should be gently encouraged to attend to your toddler in the same manner they did before the baby's arrival. One of the toughest parts for your toddler is adjusting to how the baby will pull your attention away from them, especially when you're feeding the baby and putting them to bed. Having your coparent set aside these times as special bonding times with your toddler will greatly assist with their adjustment.

**Q:** *My toddler loves to look at pictures and videos on my cell phone and watch TV. How much screen time is appropriate for a toddler?*

The American Academy of Child and Adolescent Psychiatry recommends that children between the ages of 0 and 18 months use technology or screen time only to video chat with loved ones. Having Grandma read a story over Zoom or saying goodnight to Mom while she's on a business trip are excellent uses of screen time. Between the ages of 18 months and 3 years, appropriate screen time is described as "minimal high-quality TV time." This means that the content should be educational, age-appropriate, and limited in length (about one hour). Toddler moms are encouraged to save TV time for those moments when they really need their toddler to remain occupied, such as while they're preparing dinner, caring for a sibling, or traveling on an airplane or when stress or fatigue is high. Less-than-ideal times for screens include while your little one is riding in the car (especially for a routine trip), getting ready for bed (screen time can disrupt their sleep), or dining in a restaurant (family time).

When screen time is permitted, parents should encourage television viewing rather than close-up screens, such as cell phones, tablets, or laptops. Toddlers should only be exposed to age-appropriate television shows that highlight school-readiness skills, social skills, or safety instruction (as opposed to YouTube videos or shows that don't have a beginning, middle, and end and roll from one to the next without pause). The type of screens and the content the child is exposed to can greatly impact their ability to transition away from screens, maintain sustained attention, and entertain themselves. You want screen time to be fun and enjoyable, not an instigator of power struggles with or disengagement from family or community. Screen time should be a little bonus part of a toddler's day, designed to give Mom the opportunity to carve out a few minutes of peace or productivity.

That being said, give yourself a break, Mama, if you depend on screens a little more often than you'd prefer.

## Concluding Thoughts

Remember, you are the very best mom for your toddler, even as you continue to change and grow as a parent and as a person. You've cared for your little one through sleepless nights, fevers, tantrums, snuggles, and giggles, and you ultimately know what's best for them. Read this book with the mindset of "I'm always ready to learn new ideas," but set aside what's not right for you, and ask more questions if you're unsure as to how some of the principles can be best implemented with your child. Raising a toddler is no joke, and you're not alone in this. Take a deep breath because you've got this, Mama.

# Resources

## Books

McCoy, Jazmine. *The First-Time Parent's Guide to Potty Training: How to Ditch Diapers Fast (and for Good!).* New York: Zeitgeist Publishing, 2020.

Phelan, Thomas. *1-2-3 Magic: The New 3-Step Discipline for Calm, Effective, and Happy Parenting.* Rev. 6th ed. Naperville, IL: Sourcebooks, 2016.

## Podcast

*One Day You'll Thank Me*: A parenting podcast cohosted by Dr. Tara Egan and Anna Egan, her teenage daughter

## Websites

Big Little Feelings: BigLittleFeelings.com

Raising Teens Today: Facebook page @RaisingTeensToday

# References

American Academy of Child and Adolescent Psychiatry. "Screen Time and Children." Last modified February 2020. AACAP .org/AACAP/Families_and_Youth/Facts_for_Families /FFF-Guide/Children-And-Watching-TV-054.aspx.

American Psychological Association. *Resolution on Physical Discipline of Children by Parents*. Accessed April 5, 2021. APA.org/about/policy/physical-discipline.pdf.

Belsky, Janet. *Experiencing Childhood and Adolescence*. New York: Worth Publishers, 2018.

Dewar, Gwen. "Teaching Empathy: Evidence-Based Tips for Fostering Empathy in Children." Parenting Science. Last modified August 2020. ParentingScience.com /teaching-empathy-tips.html.

Egan, Tara. *Better Behavior for Ages 2–10: Small Miracles That Work Like Magic*. Melrose, MA: Lesson Ladder, 2013.

Glicksman, Eve. "Physical Discipline Is Harmful and Ineffective." *Monitor on Psychology* 50, no. 5 (2019): 22–26.

Kagan, Jerome. *The Nature of the Child*. New York: Basic Books, 1984.

Mayo Clinic. "Bed-Wetting." October 26, 2017. MayoClinic.org /diseases-conditions/bed-wetting/symptoms-causes /syc-20366685.

Moore, M. Keith, and Andrew Meltzoff. "New Findings on Object Permanence: A Developmental Difference between Two Types of Occlusion." *British Journal of Developmental Psychology* 17, no. 4 (1999): 623–44.

Sege, Robert D., and Benjamin S. Siegel. "Effective Discipline to Raise Healthy Children." *Pediatrics* 142, no. 6 (2018): e20183112. doi:10.1542/peds.2018-3112.

Willatts, Peter. "Development of Means-End Behavior in Young Infants: Pulling a Support to Retrieve a Distant Object." *Developmental Psychology* 35, no. 3 (1999): 651–67.

# Index

# Acknowledgments

To Mo Mozuch, my fantastic editor.

To Pete Hodges, my dear husband and coparent. Thank you for always making dinner.

To Julie Clark, my right-hand woman. Thank you for always keeping Dr. Tara Egan LLC running smoothly while I bury myself in a new project.

# About the Author

**Tara Egan, D.Ed.,** is a child and adolescent therapist, a parent coach, and a public speaker. She holds a doctorate in school psychology and has specialized training in counseling and family-school relations. She is the author of two other books: *Better Behavior for Ages 2–10* and *Adolescence: A Parent's Guide*. She cohosts a weekly parenting podcast with her teenage daughter, Anna, called *One Day You'll Thank Me*. You can learn more about her products and services at DrTaraEgan.com.